FACILITATE

How to Lead a Life-Giving Small Group

Joel Comiskey

Published by CCS Publishing

www.joelcomiskeygroup.com

Published by CCS Publishing
23890 Brittlebush Circle
Moreno Valley, CA 92557 USA
1-888-511-9995

Cover design by Jason Klanderud
Editing by Scott Boren

ISBN: 978-1-935789-95-6

Library of Congress Control Number: 2018907450

CCS Publishing is the book-publishing division of Joel Comiskey Group, a resource and coaching ministry dedicated to equipping leaders for cell-based ministry.
Find us on the World Wide Web at **www.joelcomiskeygroup.com**

Table of Contents

Introduction

Silence. Carl's attempt to stimulate discussion failed. "Is there anyone else who'd like to comment on this verse?" Still no response. Carl decided it was best to break the silence by launching into a spontaneous homily of the Bible passages. "At least they're receiving God's Word," he assured himself.

I know how this leader felt. I've faced similar periods of strained silence as I have led the lessons in my own small group. I've thought to myself more than once, "Why are my own discussion times so dry?" What's the missing link?"

Many small group leaders, immersed in the battle, begin to doubt their talent and leadership skills. They blame their personality or lack of leadership gifting as being reasons for the barren lessons, the uneasiness in the group, and the fact that only a few members participate in the group discussions.

The good news is that the vast majority of small group problems are solvable. I've written this book to help you turn a dry gathering into a dynamic meeting.

Healthy Groups

When defining a small group, it's important to identify essential components, or characteristics that should be present. Life-changing small groups should have the following characteristics:

1. Upward Focus: Knowing God
2. Inward Focus: Knowing each other
3. Outward Focus: Reaching out to those who don't know Jesus
4. Forward Focus: Raising up new leaders (making disciples who make disciples)

No two small groups are exactly alike but each successful group maintains the same components: seeking God (upward focus); developing relationships with one another (inward focus); reaching out to non-Christians (outward focus); and developing new leaders (forward focus). These components allow small groups the flexibility to be effective, while at the same time achieving their goal.

Bigger is not better for small groups. Growth in size excludes growth in intimacy.[1] Unless small groups remain small, they lose their effectiveness and ability to care for the needs of each member. When two people are in conversation, there are two communication lines; that number increases to twelve when four are present. With ten people, the number grows to ninety, and when fifteen people gather, there are 210 possible lines of communication. When the group membership exceeds fifteen persons, there is very little opportunity for people to know each other intimately. It's a congregation, rather than a small group.

Teaching this Material

Many churches will teach this material in a group setting. This is the normal way to use the material, but it's not the only way.

Another way to train someone is to have the person being trained complete each lesson individually and then ask someone of the same gender to coach him or her. The coach would hold the "trainee" responsible to complete the lesson and share what he or she is learning.

I believe in multiple methods for teaching material. Not everyone can attend group-training meetings, but people still need training.

Additional Resources

Facilitate is part of a training series that prepares someone to become a mature follower of Jesus Christ. The *Training Series* is available at www.joelcomiskeygroup.com or by calling toll free 1-888-511-9995.

A more in-depth book on group dynamics is *How to Lead a Great Small Group So People Come Back*. I go into more detail about how to lead a small group meeting in that book. Both books are available at www.joelcomiskeygroup.com

Preparing Yourself

Small group leadership begins with heart preparation. A heart that is pure before God is the only foundation for leading a successful small group meeting. Without a heart for God, the meeting consists of only dry routines and rituals.

A certain winsomeness characterizes dynamic small group leaders. They demonstrate loving concern, but they firmly lead. They allow discussion to flow naturally but refuse to stray from the theme. They listen intently but won't allow one person to dominate the meeting. They build community but not at the expense of reaching out to the unsaved. They take responsibility for the group but refuse to do everything. They promote group identity but never at the expense of the multiplication of new small groups.

Does this balance sound difficult? Let's just say impossible—apart from the work of the Holy Spirit. Logic and technique, while necessary, can't teach the when and how of small group dynamics. Effective small group leadership begins with a transformed heart. The Holy Spirit works inside the small group leader so he or she can minister from the overflow of the heart.

To successfully navigate the uncharted waters that lie ahead, you'll need a guide, one who knows the way. Jesus said, "But when he, the Spirit of truth, comes, he will guide you into all truth. He will not speak on his own; he will speak only what he hears, and he will tell you what is yet to come" (John 16:13).

You don't fully understand the tears and fears of Joan or the ambitions and dreams of John.

When Joan, John, and the rest of the group arrive in your living room, the chemistry is unpredictable. You can know all the practices and techniques of small group dynamics and fail to meet the deep needs of the group. You need a guide—The Holy Spirit.

Try IT!

Read Acts 2:1:13 and 4:31

- How many times were the disciples filled with the Spirit in these passages? (and many more times afterwards)

____

____

- Why does a person need to be filled with the Spirit more than once?

____

____

Stop Preparing for the Small group

Do yourself and your group a favor. Cease all small group preparation at least one-half hour before the small group begins (e.g., lesson, refreshment preparation, etc.). Take that time to prepare your heart before God, asking Him to fill you with the Spirit. Here are some key principles to be filled with the Spirit:

- Confess all known sin. David says, "If I had cherished sin in my heart, the Lord would not have listened" (Psalm 66:18).
- Ask for the filling of the Holy Spirit. "If you then, though you are evil, know how to give good gifts to your children, how much more will your Father in heaven give the Holy Spirit to those who ask him!" (Luke 11:13). Jesus says, "Ask and it will be given to you; seek and you will find; knock and the door will be opened to you. For everyone who asks receives; he who seeks finds; and to him who knocks, the door will be opened" (Luke 11:9-10).
- Be filled with the Spirit daily. In Ephesians 5:18, Paul says, "... be filled with the Spirit." The phrase "be filled" in the Greek points to a continual, constant filling. It's a daily thing.

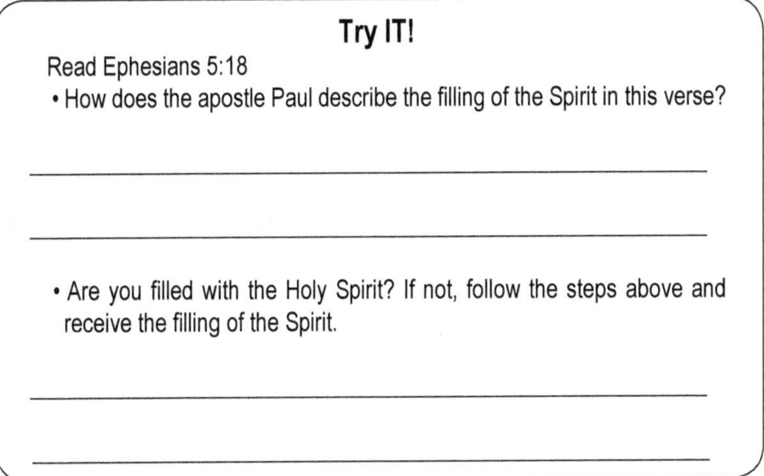

Try IT!

Read Ephesians 5:18

- How does the apostle Paul describe the filling of the Spirit in this verse?

____

____

- Are you filled with the Holy Spirit? If not, follow the steps above and receive the filling of the Spirit.

____

____

So many unexpected things happen in the course of a normal small group: the ringing phone, the unexpected non-Christian visitor, the forgetfulness of Susan to prepare the icebreaker, the broken guitar string, and John's job loss. When John shares about getting fired during the ice-breaker, should you pray for him immediately, give him more opportunity to share, or wait until after the lesson (perhaps you know John has the tendency to talk a lot)? You'll need the Spirit's wisdom.

If you're a veteran small group leader, you know plans and preparation can help—but they're insufficient. You'll agree that Spirit-anointed common sense will hit the home runs.

Following rigid, preconceived plans when someone is hurting results in a strikeout. To win the game, you need a good coach. The great news is that the Holy Spirit is willing to give to you the inside, play-by-play counsel on a moment-by-moment basis. To hear his voice loud and clear when you need it, you'll need his filling before the meeting begins.

Remember also that some of the most powerful ministry occurs while chomping on chips or eating cookies after the small group meeting. Heart talk often transpires when our guard is down, and we're not worried about every detail of the small group meeting. The Spirit might stir you to minister to the newcomer or talk with the wayward. You might feel impressed to speak to Johnny, who rarely talks during the meeting. Or maybe you need to just listen, while others lead the conversation.

Stay in tune with him, and he'll make your way prosperous. He'll guide your steps.

Christ made decisions after communing with the Father. As we read in Luke 5:16, he made it a priority to spend time alone with His Father: "… Jesus often withdrew to lonely places and prayed." Luke 5:15 explains that when Christ's fame was spreading, the success of his ministry compelled him to spend more time with God. Amid an increasingly busy ministry, he separated from the multitude for quiet time. If Jesus Christ, our model, prioritized his time with the Father, shouldn't we?

Try IT!

Read Matthew 6:12-13

• What do these verses tell us about Jesus' prayer life?

____

____

• What can you do to follow Christ's example?

____

____

As a small group leader, spending time with God must be your chief and most important priority. When your group senses you're hearing from God, they'll be more apt to follow you. When you can point to times in which you sensed his urging, and he spoke to your heart, you'll gain the respect of those in your group.

Do IT!

Commit to 30 minutes of personal spiritual preparation before the group meeting starts.

More than Techniques

This book emphasizes the importance of small group dynamics. Yet, I've warned you not to follow techniques too closely. I've said, "Let the Spirit guide you. Be open to analyze each situation with Spirit-anointed common sense." Sound like a contradiction? Not really. Plans, techniques, and diligent preparation for the small group meeting are exceedingly important. Just don't allow them to control you. That's the Spirit's job. As you spend time in his presence, you'll make better plans, know how to handle each situation, and meet the needs of those present.

Great small group leadership begins with a heart immersed in Christ and filled with the Holy Spirit. If you heart isn't right, then no list of techniques can lead your group into the things God has ahead.

Memorize IT!

„If you then, though you are evil, know how to give good gifts to your children, how much more will your Father in heaven give the Holy Spirit to those who ask him!" (Luke 11:13)

Remember it!

1. What truth from this lesson impacted you the most? ________

____

____

____

____

2. Main points:

- Stop preparing small group details at least one-half hour before the meeting starts in order to spend time with God.
- Prioritize your daily devotional life in order to hear from God.
- Depend on God more than techniques.

Apply it!

1. Treat the Holy Spirit as a person—feel his presence, talk to him, listen to him, and worship him.
2. Ask the Holy Spirit to fill you daily.
3. Live each day in humble dependence on the Holy Spirit.

Chapter Notes

Chapter Notes

How to Structure a Meeting

Nancy arrived early for the small group. She began to pour out her heart, "I'm so thankful I'm no longer living with Andy. I feel clean inside, but it's still so hard; at times, I feel like I need him." Frank and Kathy arrived in the middle of our conversation and added their own thoughts.

The Holy Spirit showed me we needed to go deeper, rather than abruptly restarting the small group meeting with an icebreaker. Tuning into Nancy's struggles and desiring to help her, all of us shared how God delivered us from similar bondages. My intended lesson topic covered anger, but I decided to talk about freedom from bondage through the power of the Holy Spirit. God moved in a mighty way that night.

On this particular occasion, I felt moved by the Holy Spirit to scrap my plans because of a unique situation. However, I did have a plan. Ninety percent of the time, I'll follow that plan. You also might feel impressed to change your plans and do something unique—just make sure you have a strategy for your small group. Great small group meetings begin well and end well. They function like our arms, connecting everything together in an appealing way.

Some small group agendas are better than others. The best agenda I've discovered is called the 4Ws: *Welcome, Worship, Word, and Witness* (or *Works*). I like this order so much because it allows the group:

- To experience the *one anothers* of Scripture. The *Welcome* time enhances the open sharing of our personal lives.
- To enter the presence of God. We approach God through the *Worship* time and receive His fullness.

- To interact with God's Word; God speaks to us through the *Word.*
- To reach non-Christians; The *Witness* time helps the group focus on outsiders.

The four Ws will not automatically produce life in your small group. They will, however, enhance God's work among the members of your group.

Try IT!

Read Luke 2:25-27

- What do these verses tell us about Simeon's spiritual life

____

____

- How can you apply Simeon's example of being 'led by the Spirit'?

____

____

Welcome (15 minutes)

Most small group members are tired when they arrive at the group. They've worked hard all day and probably don't feel like *being spiritual.* Some will attend because they know they should be there, not because they *feel like attending.*

Begin on a joyful note. Let them ease into group life.

The *Welcome* time normally begins with a dynamic question that breaks the ice. The best icebreakers guarantee a response.

You can buy entire books on lively icebreakers, so you shouldn't experience a shortage in this area.[2]

Most people know us because of our profession. We're known as a teacher, construction worker, doctor, housewife, and so forth. A great icebreaker stirs us to talk about our hobbies, family background, or personal experiences. The icebreaker draws the group together in a family atmosphere.

Some small groups even provide a light snack during the Welcome time (people feel more socially inclined when eating something). This is a great idea, if you're not on a tight budget. However, don't neglect the closing refreshment time.

Evaluation Question: When you've finished the *Welcome Time*, are group members more comfortable with each other and ready to enjoy being together?

Try IT!

Read Luke 2:25-27

- Do you have a favorite icebreaker? If so, what is it?

____

____

- If not, make up an icebreaker that you think others would enjoy and use it in your small group.

____

____

Worship (20 minutes)

The goal of the *Worship* time is to enter the presence of the living God and to give Him control of the meeting. The worship time helps the group go beyond socializing. Without Christ's presence, the small group is no different than a work party, a family gathering, or meeting friends at a football game,

Entering God's presence through song is an important part of the worship time. Make sure everyone has a song sheet. Some small groups prefer to play a YouTube video while the members follow along.[3]

The worship leader should pick two to four songs *before* the worship starts. Or the worship leader might invite small group members to select the songs *before* the worship time and then sing them in sequence. I think it's best to concentrate on God during the entire worship time, rather than stopping and starting to pick the song. I like to intermingle praise and prayer between songs.

Don't limit the *Worship Time* only to singing songs. At a small group seminar, one participant shared, "It's important to go beyond singing songs. Our group has experienced God's presence through reading Psalms together, praying sentence prayers, or even waiting in silence."

- Evaluation question: When finished with worship, is the group focused on God and ready for Him to minister to the group?

Try IT!

- Describe the worship experience you're having now in your small group?

____

____

____

____

- How does worship impact our relationship with God?

____

____

____

____

____

Try IT!

True or false:

- Worship is the natural response of a grateful heart to God's grace, mercy, and love.

____

____

- Worship can happen anytime and in any place.

____

____

- God prefers worship in a building on Sunday.

____

____

Word (40 minutes)

The Word time is when God speaks to our hearts through the Bible. Resources abound to prepare a top-notch lesson.

Many small groups follow the same theme and Scripture as the Sunday message. Even if this is the case, it's best *not* to discuss the sermon. The people should interact with God's Word, not with the sermon. If the sermon itself is the reference point, visitors and those who missed the celebration service will feel isolated.

Even though the church provides the lesson, it's essential that each small group leader examines the lesson and applies it according to the needs in the group.

Without fail, God speaks to the group through his Word and people recognize their needs. I find it very effective to ask for specific prayer requests after the lesson time. Often we'll lay hands on those with special needs.

The small group lesson, or *Word* time, normally lasts forty minutes. I like to take ten of those forty minutes to pray for specific needs of the group.

Evaluation question: Did the group share honestly and manifest vulnerability before one another? Did the group learn how to walk more obediently with Christ during the week?

Try IT!

True or false:

- The third W means Word.

____

____

- The fourth W means Witness.

____

____

- Some churches use the Sunday sermon as the base for the small group lesson.

____

____

Witness
(15 minutes)

The last part of the small group meeting, the Witness time, helps us focus on others. There is no "one way" to do this. The thought that should guide this time is *Outreach*. The type of outreach might vary on a weekly basis:

- Praying for non-Christians to invite
- Preparing a social project
- Planning for a future multiplication

- Deciding on the next outreach event for the small group (e.g., dinner, video, picnic, etc.)
- Praying for non-Christian families

The leader might ask the group, "Remember to pray for our new multiplication that will begin in two months. Pray for Frank, who needs to complete the last training course. Pray that he'll be ready to start the new small group."

During this time, you might promote and plan a social outreach project. I'm convinced that small groups are perfectly positioned to meet the physical needs of those both inside and outside the group.

A small group offers a unique, effective way to reach deeply into the heart of a non-Christian person. The New Testament church grew and prospered through need-oriented group evangelism. God is calling His Church back once again to this exciting method of outreach.

Other ideas: Reach out to the community by visiting a retirement home, ministering to street kids, or helping out in an orphanage.

- Evaluation question: When we're done, was Jesus working through us to reach others?

Were the People Edified?

During the ministry to Nancy that I shared in the introductory story, I sensed the need to talk about the Holy Spirit's filling and His power to deliver us from sin. We examined several passages that referred to the Spirit's willingness to fill us. We concluded the lesson on our knees, seeking the Prince of Peace to fill us. My wife and I then went around and laid hands on Nancy, Frank, and Kathy, praying for them to be filled with the Spirit of God. Afterwards, Frank blurted out, "How did you know I needed that lesson? It was just for me!"

Edification literally means to build up or construct. Paul says to the Corinthian church, "What then shall we say, brothers? When you come together, everyone has a hymn, or a word of instruction, a revelation, a tongue or an interpretation. All of these must be done for the strengthening [edifying] of the church" (1 Corinthians 14:26).

The issue of building-up should be the guiding principle of the small group. A successful small group meeting is one in which everyone is built up and encouraged in the faith. The standard for success is whether Christ's body went away edified—not whether or not you fulfilled the 4Ws.

Think About IT!

Practical Steps for Edification in the Small Groups

- The Small group leader must be transparent and model what he expects others to follow
- Cultivate sensitivity to the one needing edification
- Ask the members to become a vessel used by God to edify others
- Point the one being edified back to God

Focus on Christ

The focus of your small group must be Jesus. Some want to convert the group into a Bible study, others an evangelistic crusade, and still others a worship concert. Some don't think it's a *real* small group unless someone speaks in tongues or delivers a prophecy.

Lift Jesus high in your group, and he'll give you a gentle balance of study, worship, evangelism and fellowship. Perhaps one week you'll spend more time in the Word, while another week you'll tarry in the worship time.

Remember the 4Ws are not four laws. They're guidelines to help you focus on Jesus and to maximize participation. Focusing on Jesus helps provide the proper balance.

Having a winsome order won't guarantee success in the small group. It will, however, link together essential small group values such as sharing, the Word, evangelism and worship. Like gathering arms, a proven structure will provide continuity and purpose.

Sample Small Group Meeting Sample Small Group Meeting

Welcome: icebreaker questions.

- Where did you live between the ages of 7–12?
- How many brothers and sisters did you have?
- Who was the person you felt closest to?

Worship

- Read Psalm 8 aloud in unison.
- Sing "How Great Thou Art."
- Read Psalm 29: let each person read a verse in turn.
- Ask for a period of silence for one minute; encourage the members to consider the ways God has comforted them in past situations.

Word

- Read 2 Corinthians 1:3–5.
- Ask, "Share a time when you were in a crisis and God comforted you."
- After a time of sharing, then ask, "Can you recall a time when you were used by God to comfort someone else?"
- Finally, ask, "Who in our group is in need of God's comfort right now?"
- Edify one another as God opens the way to comfort one another.

Witness

- Share names and circumstances of unbelievers in our oikoses (those closest to you) who are going through deep waters.
- Discuss how we as a small group might witness to these unbelievers by becoming God's agents of comfort in their time of distress.

Do IT!

Commit yourself to leading the Word section of your current group.

Memorize IT!

"'Not by might nor by power, but by my Spirit,' says the LORD Almighty" (Zechariah 4:6).

Remember it!

1. What scripture verse stood out to you in this lesson? ______

____

____

2. Main points:
   - Great small group meetings follow a predictable pattern:
     - -Welcome (relationship building)
     - -Worship (entering the presence of God)
     - -Word (applying God's Word to our lives)
     - -Works (reaching out to others)
   - Measure the meeting by:
     - -Were the people edified?
     - -Was Christ glorified?

Apply it!

1. Memorize the four parts of the small group (4Ws). Share those four parts with someone else without referring to your notes.
2. Write down the fears you have about your own personal ability to lead a small group and compare those with your new understanding about small group leadership.

Chapter Notes

Chapter Notes

Facilitating Others

Fred diligently prepared all week for his Thursday night group.[4] At that time, I knew little about small group ministry, and I fully expected a Bible study, complete with exegesis, opinions from commentators, and illustrations. To my astonishment, Fred spoke very little that night. He skillfully drew the information from us. Although he had scrutinized the Bible passage, he led us to dig up the treasures for ourselves. He peppered us with questions that forced us to delve deeper and deeper into the text.

I left that meeting with a new appreciation for the power of participation in Bible study. I discovered that diligent lesson preparation and open sharing are not mutually exclusive.

Fred empowered our small group to discover God's Word for ourselves. Like strong legs propelling the body onwards, Fred exemplified how facilitators can encourage others to participate.

Years later I made an unexpected visit to another small group. During the lesson, the leader rattled off numerous Greek words. "Is she trying to impress me with her knowledge?" I thought to myself. She liberally quoted Bible commentators and ended up teaching 90 percent of the lesson.

When others dared to comment, she hesitantly acknowledged them. Quickly, however, she cut them off, preferring her own authoritative voice. "These poor, bottled-up group members," I mused. "They want so badly to share their souls."

Facilitators Refuse to Preach and Teach

I visited two different young professional small groups within the same month. In one, the icebreaker fulfilled its purpose—it broke down walls of indifference and helped us to know each other better. The worship carried us into God's presence and fulfilled our deep longing for God Himself.

The leader then guided each member to participate in the small group lesson. All of us explored God's Word together. Afterwards, each member expressed personal needs in the prayer time. Finally, the small group members gathered around the refreshment table to interact socially—laughing and sharing. I left that meeting edified both socially and spiritually.

In the other group, the leader clung to the mini-service mentality. He cut short the icebreaker, leaving some without opportunity to participate. After worship, we opened our Bibles. With a Bible in one hand and a document that looked like a manuscript in the other, the leader proceeded to dominate the meeting for the next 40 minutes.

My spirit grieved for the young people who were forced to sit through this service. He answered his own questions and even controlled the concluding prayer time.

This leader, like many, was so comfortable in hearing his own voice that he kept on talking and talking. Several times, I felt compelled to break into the small group meeting and open it up for discussion, but I controlled myself, not wanting to embarrass the leader. I left that night feeling "bottled up."

The effective small group leader talks only 30 percent, while the small group members share 70 percent of the time. This should be the goal of every small group leader.

Try IT!

Read James 1:19

- What does James say about listening in this passage?

____

____

____

- How can you improve your listening skills?

____

____

____

Facilitators Empower Others

The root definition of facilitator is to make easy. The synonym *empower* helps clarify what an effective leader does best. The facilitator is the group's servant, empowering the members to enjoy God and each other. Rather than lording over the group, the facilitator washes their feet, ministering to them at every opportunity.[5]

Small group facilitators encourage group members to speak what's on their minds. They gently remind the group to empower each other through active listening. The goal of the small group, in fact, is to strengthen others through mutual edification.

The facilitator might ask, "What do the rest of you think?" All members are asked to fill in the blanks and add new dimensions. After everyone has taken a turn, the facilitator summarizes the comments of the group.

Communication in a classroom takes place between student and teacher (question-answer). The teacher imparts information while the students take notes. However, communication in an effective small group flows among all group members. Elizabeth, a member of the small group, feels just as free to direct her comments to John, a group member, as she does to Jane, the group facilitator. Often the facilitator simply observes the communication that's taking place.

The facilitator is not stiff and passive—only listening and not sharing. A facilitator interacts just like other group members, sharing personal reflections, experiences, and modeling transparency.

Synonyms for facilitate include: Help, Aid, Assist, Ease, Make Easy, Empower, Lubricate, Smooth, Make Possible, Smooth the Progress

Like Fred in the opening illustration, facilitators diligently mine the riches of God's Word for the purpose of empowering the members to discover God's treasure for themselves. They know the basics of inductive Bible study, but the fruit of their study results in increased participation.

Try IT!

- Think about a small group meeting when everyone shared versus one when only the leader talked. What was the difference? How would you rate the two experiences?

____

____

____

____

Facilitators Need Supervision

Small group leaders need supervision to be successful. If you're currently leading a small group, I hope you have someone watching over you. If not, ask the senior pastor to periodically meet with you. Small group leaders benefit from interaction with more experienced leaders. Learn from the growing small group churches around the world. They don't allow small group leaders to work alone; they provide close supervision and contact.

Facilitators Learn while Leading

Don't wait too long to use your gifts and talents. You can't grow unless you exercise your gifts and talents along the way.

A farmer wanted to enter the world of horse racing, so he bought a beautiful race horse. Every day he cleaned the horse and groomed it. He didn't want to exercise the horse for fear of wearing it out, so he used his faithful mule to perform the farm chores. On the day of the big race, his prize horse could hardly move. His muscles were flabby and atrophied. The farmer had no other choice except to enter his mule for the big race.

Don't sit on the sidelines, waiting for the big race. People learn best while practicing what they're learning. Some think it's best to wait until they *really* know the Bible. "You'll never have enough Bible knowledge," I tell them. "Even recognized, highly skilled Bible teachers are learning continually."

Others think they must wait until they're ready to answer all questions. "You don't need to answer every question," I tell them. In fact, I encourage this response to difficult questions: "I'm not sure how to answer that question, but I'm going to look into it this week, and I'll get back to you." This humble stance will generate confidence between you and your small group members. During the week, you can study the Bible, read Bible commentaries, and especially go to your supervisor or pastor to ask for help.

Try IT!

Read Philippians 3:13-14

- What does this passage say about Paul as a learner?

___

___

Two Essential Qualities of Facilitators

What characteristics are necessary to lead a group?

At least two: They're summed up in the great commandments—love God and love your neighbor. All small group leaders must abundantly possess these two attributes.

Sincere Love for God

Jesus, God's Son said, "Love the Lord your God with all your heart and with all your soul and with all your mind and with all your strength"(Mark 12:30). No one has arrived at the stage of loving God completely. The key questions are: Are you growing in your love relationship with Jesus Christ? Are you enjoying his love letter to you on a daily basis? God uses people who are growing in love with him.

Sincere Love for Others

Jesus followed the first command with a second: "Love your neighbor as yourself. There is no commandment greater than these" (Mark 29:31). The time-tested, oft-quoted phrase still rings true,

People don't care how much you know until they know how much you care. Your success as a small group leader depends on your love for the small group members. More than any other attribute, God uses leaders who care. Anyone can successfully lead a small group—if he or she is willing to love people.

Do IT!

Practice the 70-30 principle in your next small group (listen 70% of the time and speak 30% of the time)

Remember to Facilitate!

Remember Fred. He fervently studied the Scripture in order to facilitate participation. He empowered others by giving them a chance to apply the Scriptures to their lives. Facilitators like Fred refuse to convert the small group meeting into another church service. The effective tools of the facilitator's craft are application–oriented, Bible-related questions, a listening ear and loving concern for all group members.

Our legs offer support and strength to the rest of the body. Likewise, the successful attributes of facilitation support and encourages each member to participate. Effective small group leaders empower others to share and apply the lesson to their own lives.

Memorize IT!

James 1:19: "My dear brothers, take note of this: Everyone should be quick to listen, slow to speak and slow to become angry."

Remember it!

1. What Scripture verse stood out to you in this lesson? ______

____

____

2. Main points:
    - Facilitators should refuse to only preach and teach
    - Facilitators empower others
    - Facilitators learn while leading
    - Two essential qualities for facilitators are:
        - Sincere love for God
        - Sincere love for others

Apply it!

1. Look up the word "facilitate" in the dictionary. Meditate on its meanings and apply its meanings in leading a small group.
2. Next time your group meets, make it a point to ask questions and listen attentively to each person.

Chapter Notes

Chapter Notes

Chapter Notes

Practicing Transparency

Successful small group leaders open their heart and soul to allow others to see who they really are. They don't hide behind outward appearances and trumped-up images. They realize by sharing weaknesses they gain strength. They create an open door that leads to more intimate group communion.

My good friend, Bill Mangham, excels in transparency. Others feel relaxed in Bill's presence because they know he's real. On one occasion, Bill walked into my home and showed me two photos. One revealed his son successfully surfing a wave; the other showed Bill falling flat on his face, as he tried to do the same. "A typical example of Bill Mangham," I thought to myself. Bill creates friends by practicing transparency. He doesn't try to impress others. In fact, I've never heard Bill boast about his accomplishments. He doesn't need to because they're so evident. Bill is respected by all and is constantly elevated to leadership positions.

Bare. Naked. This is the reality of our situation before God. The writer of Hebrews declares, "Nothing in all creation is hidden from God's sight. Everything is uncovered and laid bare before the eyes of him to whom we must give account" (Hebrews 4:13). There are many examples in the Bible of transparent living before God.

Try IT!

Read 2 Corinthians 12:10.

- Think of two areas where you feel "weak"

____

- Now meditate on how God can receive glory through each of those areas of weakness.

____

- Share transparently with the group about what God has shown you.

____

Lead the Way

Group transparency will never happen unless the leader shares some of his or her deep struggles. David Hocking says, "Learn to admit your mistakes in the presence of the group and to apologize sincerely when things go wrong or do not turn out the way you expected…admitting failure in the midst of success is a key to good leadership. Learn to be open and honest before others. They'll love you for it (or at least fall over backwards out of shock!)."[6]

If the leader always wants to give the best impression, the other small group members will do likewise. Some leaders imagine they're promoting transparency, but their testimonies don't resonate with the members. "Pray for me, I'm really struggling. Normally, I spend 4 hours in daily prayer and Bible reading, but recently I've only spent 1 hour..." How will people react? "Yea, right, like she really needs our prayers..." Most likely the majority in the group struggle to spend 15 minutes in daily devotions.

Don't wait until you have a major problem to share. What about the small, daily difficulties we all face? The breakdown of your computer, the long wait in line, or the demanding schedule at work.

When my computer broke down, for example, I shared my frustration with the group. "This has been a miserable week. I didn't reach a single objective. I was a slave to trying to get my computer running again." People could relate, and they saw me as a real person—as opposed to *Pastor* Comiskey! Ralph Neighbour says:

> We have found in Small group life that group members will typically be as transparent and open as the leader is willing to be. In other words, group members will seldom "risk" transparency and openness until they have seen someone else take the same risk... . The question is whether God would have all of us be open and vulnerable. Living in community means living in relationship, and living in relationship means vulnerability and transparency.[7]

"I don't know how to model transparency," you say. "How do I begin?" Why don't you ask the members to pray for an area of weakness or struggle in your own life? When asking a question that requires vulnerability, share first, setting the model for others to follow.

Shirley Peddy says, "Tell your story first. So often we make the mistake of asking the other person a question, and putting him on the spot. By disclosing something personal about yourself, you take the initial step toward creating trust."[8]

You don't always need to share problems, fears or weaknesses. What about your desires and plans? Transparency means talking about yourself in an honest way, allowing others to know your aspirations, dreams, and hopes.

Try IT!

Read 2 Corinthians 7:5

- What can we learn from the apostle Paul about transparent sharing?

____

Honest to Others

We've all experienced "fellowship" times when everybody tried to impress each other. You feel pressure to perform. True Christian fellowship, on the other hand, is transparent and honest. John says, "... if we walk in the light, as he is in the light, we have *fellowship* with one another, and the blood of Jesus, his Son, purifies us from all sin" (1 John 1:7).

Close relationships require intimacy. And intimacy demands vulnerability. Letting people know us at our point of need can be hard because we fear rejection if they find out about the "real" us.

John Wesley promoted open sharing as the cornerstone of his small group church in the eighteenth century. When Wesley died, he left behind a church of 100,000 members and 10,000 small groups. Wesley's small groups (called class meetings) normally lasted for one hour, and the main event was "reporting on your soul."[9]

The class would open with a song. Then the leader would share a personal, religious experience. Afterwards, he would inquire about the spiritual life of those in the group. The meeting was built upon the sharing of personal experience of the past week. Wesley's class meetings are best described by one word: transparency.

Small groups thrive with open, honest sharing. Walls of hurt crumble. Healing occurs. Churchgoers who get lost in the pews suddenly have a name and face. Statistics on a church roll become priests of the living God. Church comes to life as people share transparently in the small group and worship freely in the large group celebration.

Try IT!

- Reflect on a specific time when people shared deeply about life issues. Share about those memories.

____

____

- What can you do to generate more transparent sharing in the group now?

____

____

____

Confess Your Faults to Each Other

James, writing to a group of believers says, "Therefore confess your sins to each other and pray for each other so that you may be healed. The prayer of a righteous man is powerful and effective" (James 5:16). A certain healing takes place when we share our sins and weaknesses and then pray for one another. Mutual concern is the way to combat discouragement and other personal issues.

I admit discernment is needed. There's a time and a place for everything, and you don't need to share every detail of your life with everyone you meet. You also need to know that what you share will be kept confidential. What is shared in the group must not go beyond the group.

Although caution is in order, I've discovered that we as believers have the tendency to err on the conservative side. We expose too little of our lives, thus erecting barriers instead of entryways.

Try IT!

Read 1 John 1: 9

- Remember that this verse is directed to a small house church. How is your group practicing this verse?

____

____

____

____

- What can you do to follow the instructions in this verse in your group?

____

____

____

____

____

____

Transformation

Transparency should lead to transformation. When a someone reveals a struggle, he or she is reaching out for help. "Pray for me." "Help me." The desired result is change. "We want to stop fighting and start understanding each other," the young couple shares. Such deep sharing springs from an earnest desire to change.

The small group should hold the couple accountable to improve their behavior—not in a legislative, legalistic way, but through constant encouragement.

Think About IT!

Accountability in the Discipleship Groups of John Wesley. Questions asked at each Methodist band meeting:

- What known sins have you committed since the last meeting?
- What temptations have you met with?
- How were you delivered?
- What have you thought, said, or done which may or may not be sin?

The writer of Hebrews had transformation in mind when saying, "Let us not give up meeting together, as some are in the habit of doing, but let us encourage one another—and all the more as you see the Day approaching" (Hebrews 10:25). Transparency without transformation is superficial. We call it a *feelings time* or a *Love Boat* small group.

The person, having unburdened his soul, willfully goes right back into the mire. "I can't find time to have devotions," Jim shares. "I'm too busy." The leader might respond, "Let's pray for Jim." The group prays for transformation to take place and for Jim to see the need to place the living God before accomplishments. Yet, if Jim shares the same transparent confession week after week but doesn't take concrete steps to prioritize God in His schedule, it's right to assume he wants transparency without transformation.

Try IT!

Read James 1:22-23

- How does James describe the person who only hears God's Word?

____

- What can your group do to hold members accountable to their commitments?

____

____

Guide the Group Into Deeper Levels of Communication

A group will not be vulnerable immediately. There are steps to lead a group into deep levels of intimacy. During the initial stages, your group will share the latest weather, sports, event at church, or work-related news. Slowly, the group will enter new levels of intimacy. You, small group leader, must skillfully guide the group to these new levels.[10]

Level One:Small talk (weather, etc.). This is where casual conversation occurs—chitchat. Example: How are you today? The weather sure has been cold.

Level Two: Information or facts. During this level, members of the group exchange facts. Example: I just heard today that they're going to raise gas prices even higher.

Level Three: Ideas and opinions. In this stage, the members feel confident enough to defend ideas, knowing no one's going to discount their input. Example: I think the government should set limits on gas prices. If prices keep going up, the economy in general is going to suffer.

Level Four: Feelings: what's truly happening in our lives. On this level, group members feel confident enough to share feelings. Example: I've felt depressed all day, and I'm not sure why. This is the stage where group members share their dreams, hopes, fears and failures.

Personal transparency leads to a sense of being known for who we really are. True intimacy lies at this Level Four. Example: "I love to travel, but I struggle with the negative consequences on my family. When I came home from my last trip, I noticed my family really needed me. Pray for me this week as I travel to..."

The group will enter deeper levels as it grows in maturity. The leader is the key to guide the group to new levels and must create the atmosphere in which everyone is free to share. When asked open-ended application questions, the group members will talk about what's really on their hearts and minds.

Think About IT!

- Get to know one another.
- Maintain strict confidentiality among the group.
- Carry one another's burdens.
- Hold each other accountable.
- Model transparency in order for the members to do the same.

Live Honestly before God and Others

Transparent living begins by meeting daily with God in personal devotions and then honestly communicating with him throughout the day. Ask God on a daily basis to make you honest and transparent as you spend consistent time in his presence. After living in transparency before God, make it your goal to share your own weaknesses and trials in your daily relationships. Don't feel you always have to look good before others. Allow God to be strong in your weaknesses.

I certainly haven't arrived at being fully transparent. I still have the tendency to impress and hide behind a veneer of strength. Yet as I meditate on God's grace and realize he's glorified in my weakness, I'm encouraged to live honestly before God and others. Now it's your turn: Are you being transparent?

Effective small group leaders don't hide behind superficiality, acting like it's unspiritual to experience pain and problems. Rather, they bare their souls through honest transparency. They share deeply, motivating the rest of the group to follow their example.

Do IT!

Practice vulnerability in your group this week.

- *Share a weakness or difficulty you are experiencing.*
- *Share a victory or area where you are thankful.*

Memorize IT!

"But if we walk in the light, as he is in the light, we have fellowship with one another, and the blood of Jesus, his Son, purifies us from all sin"(1 John 1:7).

Remember it!

1. What truth stood out to you in this lesson? ______________

____

____

2. Main points:
    - The Biblical mandate to confess our faults to one another is often followed in the small group meeting.
    - The facilitator must exemplify transparent sharing
    - Transparency should lead to transformation

Apply it!

1. Prepare to share a transparent area of your life in the small group meeting. This might be a positive or negative aspect of your life.
2. Aim for transformation rather than simply information.
3. Guide the group into deeper levels of communication.
4. Find a mentor who will help you live honestly before God and others.

Chapter Notes

Chapter Notes

Chapter Notes

Asking Stimulating Questions

Recently, Peter accepted my challenge to lead four consecutive lessons. Two of them were as dry as a bone, while the others stirred exciting discussion. The difference? Peter's questions. In all four lessons, he listened intently, called individual members by name, and was careful not to dominate. On two occasions, however, he used questions that stimulated participation. Often the difference between effective discussion and the type that fizzles into embarrassed silence has to do with the type of question the leader asks.

As you train your mind to identify and prepare stimulating, open-ended questions, your small group will soar. The people will leave edified, making plans to return the next week.

Closed Questions Versus Open Questions

During the two sub-par meetings, Peter focused entirely on the Bible passage. We covered the book of Jonah, so Peter asked: "Where did Jonah flee?" "To Nineveh," a member replied. "Great answer," said Peter. "Anyone else?" Silence.

"Why did Jonah flee?" asked Peter. "Because he was disobedient," said another member. Peter tried to get more people to talk. "Would anyone else like to share?" A few mumbled a variation of the same answer, but when all was said and done, there was only one answer: Jonah was disobedient.

Peter listened well, gave positive feedback and did everything right. What more could the group say? There was basically only one answer to give. Jonah fled because he was disobedient. Someone might have added a few more adjectives like, "Jonah was gravely disobedient," but why bother? Even a superb, highly trained leader couldn't elicit more discussion from the question. Peter could have waited in silence for an hour, hoping for someone else to talk, and we'd have sat there in silence with him.

I talked to Peter a few days later. I shared with him my own failures and discoveries—especially in the area of asking questions.

Something clicked in Peter and the next lesson was excellent. We covered Psalm 46:1, "God is our refuge and strength, an ever-present help in trouble." Peter began with a few closed, observation questions to help us understand the Biblical text. Yet, this time he quickly applied the Biblical passage to our own lives, with questions like, "When was the last time you had a crisis? How did you handle it?" Peter followed with another application question, "How did God become a refuge in your life through your crisis?"

Everyone had something to share. "Many years ago, I administered the most successful tailoring business in the country," Paul began. "I loved my job and even made suits for the president. At the height of my success, the doctors told me it was either my health or my job, so I had to leave it. But God..."

Then Carol shared, "Recently, my daughter Mary said she'd be home at 10 p.m., but at 1 a.m. she still hadn't arrived. I'm a nervous person anyway, but this time I was beyond myself. Yet, through prayer God began...." Our group shared deeply that night. We bore each other's burdens. We went away edified, encouraged and eager to come back for more.

Preparing the right questions before you start the meeting can give you assurance that the discussion will be lively and dynamic. Closed questions have one correct answer. When a leader uses too many of them, he positions himself as the Bible expert who's trying to discover the brightest, most Biblically literate students.

Open-ended questions, on the other hand, elicit discussion and sharing. There is more than one right answer. Open-ended questions stir small group members to apply the Biblical truths to their own lives.

Open Versus Closed Questions	
Examples of questions that generate discussion:	Examples of closed questions that elicit one answer:
• What are you going to do differently as a result of hearing these verses? • Share your experiences concerning... • How has God spoken to you?	• Do you agree with this passage? • Who is the main character in this passage? • What does this passage say about……?

Preparing Dynamic Questions

Let's look at an example from the familiar passage in John 3:16: "For God so loved the world that he gave his one and only Son, that whoever believes in him shall not perish but have eternal life."

Observation	Interpretation	Application
Understanding what the Bible passage says.	Clarifying what the Bible passage means.	Putting the Bible passage into practice in our everyday lives.

Observation

You could start out with a closed-ended *observation* question like: "How did God demonstrate his love for us?" The answer lies within the text. In this case, you're simply asking the people to *observe* and answer what they see in the verse. Even one who had never read the Bible could answer the question: "God demonstrated his love by sending His Son."

It's great to include a few observation questions in the beginning of the small group lesson. Such questions will help your members understand the meaning of the Bible passage.

Try IT!

- Write down your own observation question from John 3:16.

____

____

____

Interpretation

You could go one step further and ask your small group members to interpret what the verse means, yet for the most part this is still a closed question. For example, you could ask: What kind of love did God demonstrate? Some might talk about God's sacrificial love; others might refer to God's Fatherly compassion.

The leader might be ready to talk about the Greek word agape, which refers to Christ's self-sacrificing love on the cross. While there is room for a few such interpretation questions to better understand the Bible, this is not the goal of the small group. If you use this type of question too frequently, your people will leave with lots of knowledge but little transformation in their own lives.

Observation and interpretation questions help us understand the Bible, but for the most part they're closed questions. They reach the head but not the heart. They can provide useful Biblical information, but they'll generate little interaction.

Try IT!

- Write down your own interpretation question from John 3:16.

____

____

____

____

Application

Let's look at an open-ended application question covering John 3:16. You could say: "Describe your experience when you first understood that God loves you." You could then call on one of the believers in the group: "Susan, would you share what happened when you first experienced God's love for you?"

This type of question/exhortation takes the well-known verse in John and invites members to apply it. Many will share. You could also ask a question like: "How did you come to know God loves you? Did someone talk to you about God? Were you alone in your room? Share your experience."

Try IT!

- Write down your own application question from John 3:16.

____

____

____

Think About IT!

Practice Group

Philippians 4:13: "I can do everything through him who gives me strength."

- Observation question: "How many things can we do through God's strength?"
- Interpretation question: "Why does this verse only apply to believers?"
- Application question: "How has Christ given you strength in this past week?"

Grab the Heart

Several years ago, I visited a small group that was discussing the parable of the unmerciful servant in Matthew 18:21-35. The small group leader asked question after question about what the text said (observation), then a few more questions about what the text meant (interpretation), but not once did he ask the people to apply these verses to their own lives.

He missed a perfect opportunity. He could have said: "Share an experience when you felt bitterness toward another person." He could have followed with: "Share how you overcame those feelings and were able to forgive that person." Most likely there were people that very night who needed freedom from pent-up bitterness and who were longing to share with others.

Make sure you grab the heart during the small group lesson. Don't allow your people to leave the group without having applied the Bible to their own lives. I know of one small group leader who likes to conclude the Word time by saying: "In light of what we've read and discussed in this passage, how do you think God wants to use this in your life or the life of this group?"

I recommend, as a minimum, one application question for every two observation/interpretation questions.

Think About IT!

Questions Worth Repeating

Questions should focus on the main meaning of the passage and its application. Here are four questions that can be used repeatedly with some variation:

- What stands out to you in this passage?

____

- What seems to be the main point of this passage?

____

- Can you illustrate this truth from an experience in your life?

____

- What is God saying to you right now?

____

____

____

Aim at Transformation

Every lesson should give people something to feel, to remember and to do. The goal of the small group is to transform lives, rather than take in knowledge. For this reason, it's great to remind small group members about last week's challenge and to determine if anything significant happened.

The leader might start the lesson time by saying, "You'll remember that last week we discussed 1 John 3:16-17. Let me read these verses again: "This is how we know what love is: Jesus Christ laid down his life for us. And we ought to lay down our lives for our brothers. If anyone has material possessions and sees his brother in need but has no pity on him, how can the love of God be in him?" Then ask, "Can anyone give a testimony about performing an act of kindness to someone during the past week?"

Just wait in silence for a few moments. If no one shares, at least they'll know you're expecting transformation from the small group lesson, rather than mere Bible knowledge. If you begin the lesson each week by asking how people acted on the previous lesson, the members will begin to look for ways to apply the lesson. This calls for vulnerability in your own life as well. If you failed to act on last week's lesson, admit it. People will appreciate your honesty.

Try IT!

Read Ephesians 4:22-24

- What does Paul tell us about the old and the new?

____

____

- In what areas do you need renewal today?

____

____

____

Explain the Passage Clearly

Although the lesson is based on questions, the members must understan the general context of the Bible passage in order to answer them.

Don't sit in silence for an hour, waiting for a response! If group members don't understand the question, their puzzled faces will reveal it. Perhaps the confusion occurred because they did not understand the Biblical context. In the minds of the hearers, the question appears to have no reason for its being asked.

I recommend, therefore, that the leader initiate the small group lesson (the Word time) by explaining the general context and meaning of the passage. The leader might use closed, observation questions to clarify the meaning, but normally it's very helpful to give a brief explanation of the passage.

There's no excuse for sloppy, superficial Bible study. Some erroneously think participatory question-based lessons don't require as much preparation time as monologue Bible studies. Wrong!

Try IT!

Read Nehemiah 8:8

- Besides reading the Bible to the people, what else did the Levites do?

___

___

___

- What kind of explanation do you give to your group of the biblical passage?

___

___

___

___

Limit Your Questions

One of the most common errors in small group agendas is including too many discussion questions. Some small group leaders feel obligated to cover all the questions—even if there are 10 or more.

A good Word time has three to five questions. If small group leaders try to cover more than that, the extroverts in the group will dominate the meeting.

My advice is to allow the people to leave with a hunger for more, rather than a commitment never to return to such a long, boring small group meeting. I also think it's important to leave time for prayer after the small group lesson. It's best to reach a crescendo of deep sharing that naturally leads to deep praying.

Try IT!

- The best small group leaders prepare excellent questions that stimulate discussion.

____

____

- What can you do to prepare great questions and then limit those questions to 3 to 5?

____

____

It's the Question

It's the question, small group leader. Just maybe, the lack of participation in your small group is the result of too many closed-ended questions. Before becoming too discouraged, thinking you lack communication skills, examine the types of questions you've been using. Begin to make sure you include open-ended application questions toward the beginning of your small group lesson, and watch your small group come to life.

Successful small group leaders use their minds to create stimulating application questions that promote participation. They realize the wording of the question often makes the difference between success and failure in promoting life changing group discussion.

Do IT!

Read Philippians 4:13.

- *Prepare a small group lesson of 3-5 questions with at least two open-ended application questions.*
- *Ask a small group leader or supervisor to review it (and be ready to use your lesson in a small group).*

Memorize IT!

"Do not conform to the pattern of this world, but be transformed by the renewing of your mind. Then you will be able to test and approve what God's will is—his good, pleasing and perfect will" (Romans 12:2)

Remember it!

1. What truth in this lesson stood out to you the most? ______

____

____

2. Main points:
   - Open-ended questions are preferable to closed-ended questions.
   - Apply the Bible through application questions.
   - Aim at transformation rather than information.
   - Explain the passage clearly in order to apply it.
   - Limit the number of questions to approximately five.

Apply it!

1. Prepare 3-5 transformational questions that grab the heart
2. Explain the passage clearly and then facilitate a lesson that stimulates discussion and application

Chapter Notes

Chapter Notes

Chapter Notes

Listening Ears

President Theodore Roosevelt, known as a man of action, was also a great listener. He expected this quality in other people. Once, at a gala ball, he grew tired of meeting people who returned his remarks with stiff, mindless pleasantries. So, he began to greet people with a smile, saying, "Murdered my grandmother this morning." Most people, so nervous about meeting him, didn't even hear what he said. But one diplomat did. Upon hearing the president's remark, he leaned over and whispered to him, "I'm sure she had it coming to her!"

Fine-tuned, listening ears are a rare commodity. It's far easier to partially listen, while wandering off into our own dreams and plans. I believe, in fact, that listening, more than talking, distinguishes effective communicators from the rest.

Most of us are so filled with our autobiography that we really don't attempt to understand the other person's point of view. We first want others to understand us. Great listeners seek *first to understand.*

Facilitative speaking involves the use of questions and suggestions to encourage further exploration: "John, I hear you saying you need to communicate more in your marriage. All of us here tonight can relate to this. John, how do you think you could start improving your communication?"

The Member's Response Takes Priority

In the small group, the *needs of the members* guide exciting lesson times.

What you have to say, leader, is not as important as the thoughts of those present! Focus on them, not on yourself, and everyone will leave edified. The best gift you can give your members is to listen intently.

When the leader has listened intently to the answer, the group will know it. A sense of satisfaction will fill the room. Perhaps a moment of silence will settle on the group. That's okay. You don't need to say anything because the fruit of listening well will present itself. The next point in the discussion flows naturally.

Try IT!

Read Proverbs 18:13

- How does the writer describe someone who doesn't listen well?

____

____

- On a scale of 1–10, how would you describe your listening skills at this moment? What do you need to do to improve?

____

____

Listen Actively

Active listening is vigorous, energetic and diligent. It requires listening to every word, like a heat-seeking missile homing in on an enemy aircraft. It takes hard work and diligent effort to think about someone else's interest more than your own.

Stephen Covey said, "Most people do not listen to understand; they listen in order to answer. While the other is talking, they are preparing their reply."[11] Most of us are accustomed to pseudo-listening. We nod our head, as if we're listening, while our thoughts might be in another, altogether different meeting. It's tempting to think about the next question, the ringing telephone, or the hassles at work.

Great leaders listen to every word the person says—to the very end. I know it's hard, but when the small group members recognize the active listening skills of the leader, they'll follow his example..

Listen to What is Not Said

The science of kinesics—or *body language*—is the study of nonverbal communication. Since 60 percent of all communication involves body language, it's important to listen to what is *not* said.

Gestures, like a bored looked, an incredulous stare, or a humorous glance to a friend, express what a person is thinking.[13]

I've witnessed hurried small group leaders demonstrate their distraction when someone's responding. It might be a gesture, a look at the watch, or a quick look at the next question. But the non-verbal message rings loud and clear: what you're sharing is either unimportant, wrong, or inappropriate.

Think About IT!

Non-Verbal Check for Small Group Leaders

When someone answers a question, do you normally respond with:

- A smile
- A nod of the head
- An offer to help

Or, unconsciously, do you:

- Have a scowl on your face
- Show little responsiveness
- Delay acting upon the needs of those present

The leader's own responsiveness through actions and gestures will set the tone of the small group meetings.

Think About IT!

- Tip one: Be transparent. If you're tired, had a bad day, or are wrestling with something, just let the group know. Your transparency will stimulate others to freely share as well. Otherwise, your small group members might think you're angry with them. The small group is the time to share reality and not to hide.

A wise leader might say, "Linda, you look like you're thinking about something. Do you have something to add?" "Well, now that you mention it, I did want to say something."

How did this small group leader know Linda wanted to say something? He observed her sitting on the edge of her chair, rubbing her chin, tapping her foot. He read her body language.

Think About IT!

Non-verbal Listening

To stimulate conversation by participants:

1. Keep an open body position (do not cross your arms or legs toward group).
2. Lean forward to show interest.
3. Nod and smile to show agreement.
4. Make brief eye contact to encourage conversation from a quiet person.

Listen to Your Members about Your Leadership

Whenever I teach a seminar or course, I ask the participants to evaluate my ministry. Often, I must force myself to read the evaluations, because I don't like to receive criticism. But I know I'll never get better unless I know how to improve. Evaluations point out weak areas and highlight strong ones.

Small group leaders listen in order to improve the quality of the small group. And the consequences of listening are far more than inheriting earthly possessions. Eternal treasures are at stake.

I'd advise you to ask your small group members how you can improve your leadership. Ask them if their needs are being met in the small group. Ask them if there's something you can do to improve the group atmosphere. Listen to them.

Try IT!

Read Proverbs 15:31

- What does this verse say about correction?

____

____

- How are you doing in this area?

____

____

Listening through Repetition

I've learned the power of clarifying and restating what group members say. One night we were discussing 1 Timothy 4:12, "Don't let anyone look down on you because you are young, but set an example for the believers..." After a few observation questions, I asked, "Can you share about a time when your example influenced someone else?"

Christina started, "In high school, my friends mockingly named me "pastor." Yet, as time passed, they came to me for counsel and soon I began a small group on campus with those same name-callers."

I responded, "Your example attracted those who mocked you and you were able to counsel them and minister to them. Great example. Others?"

Refuse to Answer Your Own Questions

"What does verse four tell us?" John asked the group. Silence. "Does anyone want to share with the group what verse four means?" More silence. "Well, let me share with you what it means..." Ineffective facilitators quickly convert into preachers at the first signs of silence.

When you ask a question, you've placed the ball in the court of the members, and now expect them to reply. When the small group leader embarks on an impromptu explanation, small group members feel cheated. "I thought he wanted me to share," a member inwardly fumes. "Why does he dominate so much?" another thinks. Many small group leaders feel insecure while waiting for a reply.

When you answer your own questions, you communicate that an answer isn't expected. They'll think, "He's only baiting us with an initial question, but he really wants to answer it himself." People will even stop responding altogether.

The leader has already spent lots of time meditating on the questions, studying the passage, and looking at the possible responses. The small group member has just heard the question for the first time. Many thoughts are bombarding the member's mind:

- "What does the Bible passage really mean?"
- "How should I answer this question?"
- "My answer is too obvious."

Then finally, the light turns on, "That's it, I have it, I think I'll share."

The first few seconds after launching the question is a time of digestion. Give the members time to chew on the question.

While the small group member is rehearsing the response, the small group leader might be anxiously thinking:

- "Was this a good question?"
- "Did I express the question correctly?"
- "How come no one's responding?"
- "Should I call on someone?"
- "I wish there was more participation,"

When someone does finally share, the small group leader feels relieved. Relax! Give your people time to think and respond. Ralph Neighbour offers this wise counsel:

> I learned years ago to briefly introduce the topic to the group and then stare at the toe of my shoe. By doing so, I was indicating that I would no longer control what happens. After a period of silence, someone invariably speaks. He or

> she probably addresses me as they do so, but I deliberately do not establish eye contact. The group realizes that I have released them and will not guide the discussion. In that freedom, the body members begin to listen for the voice of the Head, Jesus, instead of the voice of the facilitator. What happens next can be awesome![14]

One response per question is a poor ratio. Wise small group leaders want more; they ask the group for additional responses. Some small group members are introverted and must gather courage to break through their own sound barrier in order to say something.

Try IT!

Read Luke 9:28-36

- Notice verse 33, especially the last part. Like many, Peter felt he had to say something

____

____

- How do you normally respond when there's silence?

____

____

- How can you improve your listening skills when there's silence?

____

Listen Empathetically before Advising

Often people come to a small group to receive healing. They're filled with pent-up emotions and hurts: wounds from careless criticism or judgment; rejection in childhood; a failing marriage. Some have been hurt time and time again and are looking to the small group for some type of affirmation. They need close community where they can grow, receive care and slowly heal.

At some point, the person might find the courage to really share with the group (level four-transparent communication). This type of openness requires courage, guts. Those who step out on a limb to share transparently must know the limb won't be cut down. The group's response will either stimulate healing or rejection.

Most people intellectually understand their problems. Why do they share them? Because they're looking for a listening ear, a chance to be heard.

Instead of listening and empathizing with the person, certain ones have the tendency to hop on Biblical horses and plunge spears into the person. After all, isn't God holy and doesn't he hate sin! Yes, but we're not God! Remember the compassion he's had for us. We must do likewise.

When someone is facing a crisis, it's not the moment to say, "You just need to trust in the Lord. Don't you know that all things work together for good to those who love God, to those who are called according to His purpose?" This advice, while 100 percent correct, will do more harm than good to a hurting, grieving person.

Before advice, the person first must know that God's people will help bear the burden. He or she is longing for a listening ear—not a quick Biblical response. Roberta Hestenes says, "Far too often, group members are quick to offer advice to problems instead of carefully listening. This type of advice-giving often does more harm than good."[15]

I believe there needs to be a moment of silent understanding, after the burden is shared. As the members empathize with the person, godly counsel will ensue: "Joan, I can relate to your fears and doubts brought on by your friend's cancer. When my brother faced brain cancer, I felt those same fears. I wrestled for days, wondering why God would allow it. But then God showed me ..." The scales of past wounds will peel away and the new creature in Christ will appear as the small group ministers through empathetic listening.

Small group leader, advise your group to listen, rather than quickly responding with pat answers. Then demonstrate what you want them to do by your actions. People won't follow what you say; they'll follow what you do. Preparing a healing community may take some time, but it's worth the wait.

Think About IT!

Listening and Giving Advice

Helpful listening responses:

- Paraphrasing (restating in your own words what you heard the person say).
- Short affirmations ending in ways that open the door for the other to share more

Unhelpful listening responses:

- Reassuring them that they don't have much of a problem (this implies that you disagree with their judgment that they have a problem, which makes them stop talking).
- Sending quick advice (we don't know the situation).

How to tell if others want your ear or your advice:

- Watch their body language when you send advice.
- Keep your responses short, letting them choose what to talk about. Do they continue to unload their troubles, change the subject, or pursue your counsel?

Do IT!

The next time someone shares a need, resist the temptation to offer immediate advice. First show empathy and then share Scripture based on how God has ministered to you (2 Corinthians 1:3-4).

The Essence of Listening: Others

Paul advised the church in Philippi, "Do nothing out of selfish ambition or vain conceit, but in humility consider others better than yourselves. Each of you should look not only to your own interests, but also to the interests of others" (Philippians 2:3-4). He then added, "I hope in the Lord Jesus to send Timothy to you soon, that I also may be cheered when I receive news about you. I have no one else like him, who takes a genuine interest in your welfare. For everyone looks out for his own interests, not those of Jesus Christ." Paul rejoiced in sending Timothy to the church because he knew that Timothy would truly focus on the needs of those present (Philippians 2:19-21).

This quote clarifies the leader's job: "Others, Lord, yes others, may this my motto be, help me to live for others, that I might be like thee."[16] Active listening allows a small group leader to express love in a practical way. When small group members know the leader is a good listener, they'll share more freely and consistently.

Memorize IT!

"Each of us should please our neighbors for their good, to build them up" (Romans 15:2).

Remember it!

1. What stood out to you in this lesson? ____________________

____

____

2. Main points:
   - The member's response takes priority over your own.
   - Listen to what is not said (gestures, etc.).
   - Ask the group for additional responses after one person has shared.
   - Limit advice giving in the group (rather, practice empathetic listening).

Apply it!

1. Practice active listening (truly hearing what the person is saying).
2. Refuse to answer your own questions.
3. Listen to feedback from the members about your leadership.

Chapter Notes

Chapter Notes

An Encouraging Tongue

It's no accident that the words "community," "communion," and "communication" all sound alike. These words share common roots from the Latin words for *with* and *one*. They involve being *with one another* and being one *with each other*. It's all about communication that leads to communion. Small groups enable the laity to communicate God's Word and apply it to their own lives, thus growing in community with God and others.

Small group leaders edify with their mouths, thus creating the atmosphere of transforming community. Their goal is to build-up, edify, and in the process, transform their hearers.

A good friend of mine once said to me, "I've seen so many meetings that have been correctly led from a technical point of view but lack any power because the people do not have any relationship." Is it possible to know all about how to listen, ask questions, facilitate, share transparently and still fail in the small group? I believe so. The goal of communication is community—not technical perfection.

Great Communication Encourages

I'll never forget the meeting in which one small group leader offered a slight criticism to every response. "You almost have it," James said. Another person responded to the answer and James retorted, "No, that's not it, but you're getting closer." The dance to find the right answer continued. "This is like a high school quiz," I thought to myself. As James reached the last few questions, the participation ground to a screeching halt. No one wanted to risk embarrassment.

You can always find something good in each reply. The fact that the member dared to speak is positive.

Give the person credit at every opportunity. Affirm the idea-giver, even if you can't fully endorse the idea. Thank the person for the comment, regardless of its rightness or wrongness.

Even if an answer is not based on Scripture (off doctrine), thank the person for the response and read the passage in Scripture that reveals the truth. Or say, "Thanks for your response. I'm going to do some more study on this topic, I'd like to share my findings next week."

UCLA basketball coach John Wooden told players who scored to smile, wink, or nod to the player who passed them the ball. "What if he's not looking?" asked a team member. Wooden replied, "I guarantee he'll look." Everyone values encouragement and looks for it—especially when the leader is a consistent encourager.

Try IT!

Read Ephesians 4:29.

- What kind of words should come out of our mouths?

____

____

- How can you apply this verse in your own life? How should you respond to the group members during the lesson?

____

____

Dealing with the Talker

The small group offers a warm environment in which open sharing thrives. This is extremely positive, but danger lurks as well. Some people gravitate to small groups in order to express their opinions, however negative and combative they may be.

They take advantage of the warm atmosphere to unload on others, to find a vent for their insecurity. These people love to hear their own voices. Their own insights, they think, far exceed anyone else's. No one has an opportunity to contribute while they are talking, and group members will come to resent their comments and behaviors.

Dealing with dominate talkers is probably the greatest challenge in small group meetings. I've said repeatedly that small group leaders shouldn't dominate the group. This also means, however, that one or two group members must not dominate.

The small group leader is the gatekeeper—the protector of the flock and must realize that if he permits one person to dominate the meeting, the freedom of expression of individual members will suffer.

As a small group leader, I have struggled with dedicated talkers and have constantly had to stay on top of the situation. I've often wavered between two competing emotions. When I've tried to use extra love, I've felt trampled on. Yet, when I've sought to control the talker, I've felt unloving and uneasy. Here are some practical steps to overcome this problem:

One of them is to sit next to the talker in order to give less eye contact. Talkers don't need lots of encouragement. They might even feel that you, the leader, are encouraging their nonstop conversation by eye contact, nods and a listening ear. Sitting next to the person and avoiding eye contact will signal that you're not encouraging him or her.

Call on other people to give their opinions. When you call on a person by name, you're saying to the rest: "*Wait your turn.*" For example, Jim has been dominating the conversation for the last two questions during the lesson time. For the next question, call on Judy to give the answer. When she's finished, call on Mark for an additional reply. By calling on individuals by name, you're assuming leadership responsibility and directing the conversation of the group.

Redirect the conversation away from the talker, if he or she pauses. Granted, this is a more drastic measure. When I share this tactic at a small group seminar, the crowd roars with laughter. They can just picture the small group leader waiting for the talker to take a deep breath to give someone else a chance. Although hilarious, it depicts something very serious—one person dominating the group discussion. Leaders must shield the small group from such control.

Talk directly with the person. Often, talkers simply don't understand the purpose of a small group. They sincerely think others benefit from their constant input and spiritual wisdom. They've never realized the purpose of the small group is to allow everyone to participate and share. Talking directly with the person, after or before the small group meeting will often solve the problem. Christ taught us the Father's plan of going to the person individually when he said, "If your brother sins against you, go and show him his fault, just between the two of you. If he listens to you, you have won your brother over" (Mt. 18: 15). When going personally to the talker, explain the importance of participation by all members in the group.

If the problem persists, talk to the person directly over you (e.g., coach, supervisor, zone pastor, or lead pastor). Most likely that leader has more experience in dealing with such issues and can offer valuable insight to resolve the conflict.

Ask the person to help you make the meeting more participatory by all members. I gave a small group seminar in New Jersey and afterwards a successful small group leader approached me saying, "I've found a great way to deal with the constant talker that works every time." He continued, "Ask the talker to help you get others talking." This advice makes sense. When the talker understands the larger reason for the small group and even how to participate in fulfilling this goal, it's likely the person will change.

Try IT!

- Which of the above suggestions for silencing the talker do you like best?

____

- Why?

____

____

Keeping the Communication Lines Open

The Apostle Paul faced conflict in the churches he started. He exhorted two people in the church in Philippi to make peace with each other, "I plead with Euodia and I plead with Syntyche to agree with each other in the Lord"(Phil. 4:2). For whatever reason, they were causing dissension in the house church in Philippi. Matthew Henry points out the following:

> Sometimes there is need of applying the general precepts of the gospel to particular persons and cases. Euodia and Syntyche, it seems, were at variance, either one with the other or with the church; either upon a civil account (it may be they were engaged in a lawsuit) or upon a religious account—it may be they were of different opinions and sentiments.[17]

Most of us live by the maxim, "Avoid conflict at all costs." But conflict and disagreement will happen no matter what you do or how well you do it. A Chinese proverb declares, "The diamond cannot be polished without friction, nor the man perfected without trials."

Imagine a small group with a sign on the front door, "Conflict is Expected and Welcome!" Most of us would panic when we saw that sign, but in reality, a small group often runs more like a hospital than a country club.

Think about IT!

Why do conflicts exist in small groups?

- Each person arrives with a different set of expectations of what will happen or not happen in the small group. One might expect in-depth Bible study, mountain-top worship, spiritual warfare, analytical counseling, a charismatic believer's session, or an evangelistic campaign. When individual expectations are not met, conflict ensues.
- Certain personalities do not mix well. Just because a person is a Christian doesn't guarantee he or she will mesh well with other believers.
- People in the group participate in different ways. Passive members and dominant members participate so differently that conflict might arise.
- Some small group members might not agree with the leadership style of the one leading the group. Perhaps they're more domineering, decisive or democratic, while tending to judge those leaders who lead differently.

Conflict can lead to improved conditions and growth. It can reveal the group's hidden values, and assumptions that need to be examined. When people in the group know they can express both positive and negative feelings, their group experience will be genuine. New levels of understanding should result as the group addresses differences. Fisher and Ellis paraphrase, "The group that fights together stays together."[18]

What's the best way to deal with people in conflict?

First, recognize the problem. Ignoring or hiding conflict will only confuse members. Most members will sense that conflict exists, so why hide it. You might say to an angry member, "I sense you're upset. We need to deal with this difference of opinion." Conflict can't be dealt with until it's recognized and brought into the open. An example of an opening statement might be the following:

> It seems to me that you are both feeling quite upset about your differences on this issue. I hear you both stating your position with passionate conviction, but I'm not sure that you're really listening to each other because I hear no one stopping to paraphrase or acknowledge common ground. I'd like to suggest that we back up for a moment and clarify where you agree and disagree with each other. Are you willing to do that?[19]

Second, pray. You won't solve the conflict without concerted prayer. You need to pray for wisdom and discernment.

Third, talk privately to each offending party. If both individuals decide to stay in the group (and that's unlikely in the long run), you can't allow their argument to polarize the group or create an uncomfortable atmosphere. You need to talk with each of them separately and be very clear about the rules for participation in the group. If the feud continues, treat them as unrepentant individuals continuing in sin.

If the issue is between you and someone else in the group, it's best to confront the person individually, using the Lord's own pattern: "If your brother sins against you, go and show him his fault, just between the two of you. If he listens to you, you have won your brother over"(Mt. 18:15). As the leader, if you notice conflict between two members, encourage them to talk privately to each other. Unresolved conflicts are liabilities. Few things undermine a group faster than members growing frustrated with one another.

Fourth, Impress on members the importance of listening to each other. Research in communication has repeatedly found a tendency among conflicting parties to distort or omit information during times of heated disagreement. You can help solve this problem by asking them to engage in active listening, with empathy for the other person's unique experiences and situation. Help them to criticize ideas, not people. Achieve understanding of all points of view. Deal with all emotions and feelings.

Fifth, include only those who are immediately affected. Some disagreements are better handled outside of the group meeting. Deal "off-line" with the person or persons concerned. Admittedly, there are times when the entire group should be involved in the problem solving. But try to keep it controlled and resolution-focused, with only those people who need to be restored in relationship.

Try IT!

Read Matthew 18: 15-17

- What does this passage tell us to do when someone offends us?

____

____

- What is your normal response when someone offends you?

____

____

- How can you improve in this area?

____

____

Communication Without Walls

Don't take the difference of opinion in the group as an attack on your leadership or personality. Separate yourself from the thought, the idea. By welcoming the difference of opinion, you'll sharpen your own understanding. When others in the group have differing opinions, the leader should view this as an honest opportunity to understand another point of view, not as a threat to authority. Use different viewpoints to expand the topic. Take advantage of diverse perspectives to expand the discussion and be thankful people are contributing.

My friend René Naranjo embraces the different opinions in his group. He knows non-Christians need space before coming to Jesus. They need to feel accepted, even with their opposing point of view. Through unconditional love and acceptance, he has seen dozens of non-Christians slowly accept Jesus. Doubters in his group are often melted by the love of Jesus as they continue to attend meetings.

Remember that effective communication builds community. As your small group learns to communicate more effectively—despite conflict—you'll grow in community with God and others.

Think about IT!

Three Right Ways to Respond to a Wrong Answer

- Take the blame for miscommunication: "I guess I didn't state that question very clearly—what I'm really asking is...
- Give an example: Here's an illustration of what I mean...
- Allow others to correct by giving the right answers: "Ummmm. What do the rest of you think?"

Communication Tips That Build Community

The writer of Hebrews says, "And let us consider how we may spur one another on toward love and good deeds. Let us not give up meeting together, as some are in the habit of doing, but *let us encourage one another*—and all the more as you see the Day approaching" (Hebrews 10: 23-25).

Start showing this care from the moment someone walks in the door. A smile or a hug is the best. When I visited Tony's small group, I arrived before anyone else. Tony met me at the door, gave me a big hug, offered me some refreshment, and politely excused himself for a few moments. I felt welcomed. Tony could have looked at his watch, given me a worried look, and pointed me to a seat, as he took care of his responsibilities. Instead, he made me feel welcome. He demonstrated genuine care and concern.

Respond enthusiastically to people throughout the meeting (e.g., lesson, worship, prayer, icebreaker, and vision casting). Remember that enthusiasm is not just reserved for people with bubbling personalities. It's possible to have a melancholic personality and demonstrate enthusiasm.

Pray for your small group members during the week (if possible, do it daily) and then tell them you've been praying for them. They can't hear this enough. People feel protected and loved when they know their small group leader has been praying for them.

Ask questions about their personal lives. Normally the best time to do this is immediately before or after the meeting. Ask them about their family, work, dreams and visions. On Sunday, when you see them at church, make it a point to greet them and care for them. Without even knowing it, you're fulfilling the role of a pastor by caring for your sheep.

Be aware of any physical needs and seek to meet them. My wife and I were probably the only ones in our church who knew Paul and Elizabeth were hurting physically. During the prayer time in our small group, they shared their personal needs, and we came face to face with their desperate condition. We felt led by God to help them financially, further cementing our relationship with them.

Share part of your own life with them. I love computers and computer-related activity. I brought one of my small group members (whom I had the privilege of praying with to receive Jesus) into my home office after a small group meeting one night. I showed him how to make a web page and even signed him up for his own web site. This helped establish a fast friendship between us. It catapulted us into a new dimension of sharing. Now, we weren't only talking about "spiritual things" in the small group, but were sharing our interests, our hobbies with one another. One small group leader wrote, "A woman in our small group had just undergone back surgery and was recuperating in the hospital. After a call to her, we decided to go and visit her instead of having our regular meeting at home."[20] This group was clear about its priority: community first.

Contact them outside of the small group. I'm referring here to a phone call, a note of appreciation, a cup of coffee together, or a formal visit. Your effort in getting to know the small group member outside the group will pay rich dividends later. You'll build loyalty between you and the person.

By example, the leader can guide the group to new levels of communication using principles such as restating the idea, dealing with conflict, and offering encouragement.

Try IT!

What encourages you the most?

- an act of service that makes you feel special
- a gift
- words of encouragement
- affection manifested in physical or tangible ways

Do IT!

Think of a specific encouragement for someone in the group and then deliver it.

Memorize IT!

"And let us consider how we may spur one another on toward love and good deeds" (Hebrew 10:24).

Remember it!

1. What was the main thing you learned from this lesson? ____

____

____

____

2. Main points:

- Great communication encourages others to par-ticipate.
- Don't allow certain people to dominate the meeting. Learn how to deal with those who talk too much.
- Conflict is normal and natural in a small group. Learn how to deal with it.

Apply it!

1. Have group members take turns saying three encouraging things about the other members of the group
2. Read Matthew 18:15-17, explaining the importance of talking directly to people when offended rather than gossiping. Be the first to practice this truth in your own life.

Chapter Notes

Chapter Notes

Chapter Notes

Eyes that See the Details

I once heard a professor share some wise counsel with a group of preachers: "On Sunday morning, *before* you ascend to the holy pulpit to preach God's inerrant Word before a waiting, hungry congregation, *take a moment to make sure that your pants' zipper isn't down.*" He knew the main point would be missed if the details were left undone.

Take a moment to view the details. Effective small group leaders glance around the room to make sure the song sheets are distributed, the phone is off the hook, and the chairs are arranged in a circle.

Details matter. They matter to God and they matter to your people. Imagine the incredible detail of the Old Testament Tabernacle. God asked Moses to follow His plan precisely, down to the small, seemingly insignificant details.

Atmosphere of Home

We get accustomed to the smells in our homes, but visitors sense them immediately. Smells from sources like pets, things children spill in odd places, heavy perfumes, the evening dinner, even room deodorizers, can irritate noses. You know all about your home. You like its smell. But others might not enjoy them. Think about their noses.

If you have young kids, dispose of the dirty diapers before the meeting starts or take the hamper of laundry to the washing room. God wants us to be one in Christ, but don't purposely test the oneness of your small group members by allowing strange smells to flood the room.

Make sure to clean the guest bathroom before the small group begins. Is there toilet paper, soap, a towel in place?

Try IT!

Read Mark 10: 43-45

- What is the main point of these verses?

____

____

- How can you apply the principle of servanthood to house preparation for guests?

____

____

Temperature and Lighting

The temperature in the home increases as more people are packed into a room. Members can become agitated and uncomfortable for the lack of fresh, cool air. If your people must wear heavy coats in your house, although you're in the heat of summer, you probably need to adjust the temperature. The main thing is that you're sensitive to the needs of those in the room.

One expert advised that 67 degrees is an ideal temperature for home groups.[21] Common sense is probably a better temperature gauge.

The lighting should be bright enough for everyone to read, but low enough to provide a cozy setting. If it's too dark, people will have a harder time following the worship sheets and other handouts. You may feel this is unimportant, but details do matter. It's the little things that often make the difference between an unacceptable and acceptable environment for a group meeting.

Seating Arrangement

Arrange the seating so each person can see every other person in the group. A circle is the best choice.

As the leader, place your chair so it's on the same level as the rest of those in the group—neither at the focal point nor in the background.

If your house is spacious, it's best to move the chairs into a close circle, thus occupying only a portion of the room.

Just remember that large rooms may be excellent for large groups, but they kill discussion in small groups. When people are spread far apart (as is the case in large houses), it's harder to openly share thoughts and feelings.

Some people feel intimidated about opening their homes because they're not as large or luxurious as those of other church members. Don't listen to this argument.[22] Actually, a small apartment or home generates closeness and reminds the group that, at eight to twelve people, it's time to prepare for a new group.

Think About IT!

Most house churches during the time of the first century were small. Some scholars estimate the early church houses could seat between six to fifteen people. In fact, most house churches met in apartments. Wayne Meeks, expert on the urban conditions of the early church, writes, "In Rome, most people lived in small apartments called insulae, in poor conditions with a high rental fee."[23]

Materials

I have never handed out lessons to each member. I simply invite them to follow along in their Bibles and then ask them relevant questions that apply to the text of Scripture. I do recommend printing out song sheets for everyone. They'll thank you for it. I've been in small groups where there were only a few song sheets. I shared a song sheet with the person next to me, whom I didn't know. I found myself concentrating more on holding the music steady than on worshipping Jesus. Spend the extra money and make sure everyone has his or her own copy.

Refreshments

I mentioned earlier that some small groups provide chips and dip during the icebreaker time *and* after the final prayer. If you can financially afford both, great. If you have to choose, serve refreshments afterwards.

After the meeting, we sometimes serve the people while they're still seated. Most of the time, we stand around the dining room table. This gives the most freedom for people to move around, talk freely, and visit individually. On rare occasions, we'll sit down as a group at the dining room table.

The eating of refreshments normally lasts about 15 minutes. Afterwards, people will drift out at their own pace.

However, it's the small group leader who sets the tone. If the small group leader is open to it, the people may stay for more than an hour. If the small group leader needs a cut off time, the people will know it.

Our group *normally* spends one-half hour fellowship time after the small group. My small group starts at 7:30 p.m. and ends at 9 p.m., and the people normally leave about 9:30 p.m. (there are exceptions, of course, to any rule). Depending on your personality, you may desire more or less time afterwards.

Sensitive small group leaders take advantage of this time to make personal contacts, greet visitors, and to reconfirm previous decisions. Be proactive during this time. Don't wait until people come to you. Go to them.

Think About IT!

- Don't allow providing refreshments to become a burden—or worse yet, a point of competition. If you have trouble financially and need help with refreshments, by all means ask other members of the group to contribute.
- When David Cho first started small groups in his church, he noticed competition among small group members to top last week's refreshment time. Finally, Pastor Cho had to make it a rule to only provide a simple, non-costly dessert.

Children in the Small group

I hesitate even talking about this as a *detail* of small group ministry. In truth, a whole book could be written on children's small groups, and in fact I've written a book on children in small groups.[24]

The ages of the children make a world of difference. If children are six or under, they'll need more activities, such as singing, games, visual aids or videos. This age group will obviously not benefit as much from an adult group. My preference is for children to begin experiencing small group life at a young age.

Here are a few suggestions on how to meet children's needs:

- Allow the children to stay in the adult small group for the icebreaker and worship time. During the Word time, the children can leave the adult small group and receive a personalized Bible lesson directed by one of the small group members (if necessary, the members can rotate in teaching this time). It also works to show a Christian video at this time.
- When the group consistently has four or more children, pray that God provides an adult or teenager who desires to lead a children's small group. This might be someone from your own adult small group, or from your church. The children can then meet with their small group leader in a different room of the same house for the entire small group meeting (or at least for the lesson part). This is a normal, permanent children's small group that promotes a similar small group order—icebreaker, worship, lesson, prayer and outreach. The church should provide material for the children's small group leader and all the support necessary.
- Another option is to hold small groups for children in various neighborhoods around the city. An adult would lead this small group. These afternoon small groups are a lot like the small groups of *Child Evangelism Fellowship*.

Try IT!

Read Matthew 19:14-15

- What does Jesus say about children in these verses?

____

____

____

____

- How can you apply these verses to your small group?

____

____

____

Distractions

Turn off telephone ringers and mute the volume on your answering machine. Put pets in another room or outside. Turn off TV sets, radios and computers during a meeting. Yes, our lives are busy all the time, but during the 1 ½ hours of the small group, you should focus on the small group 100 percent. Don't answer the phone.

My wife and I have made a deal to let the phone ring even if it's a small group member saying he or she will arrive late. Does it really matter if the small group has already started? Just let the person arrive when he or she arrives. You need to concentrate on those who are there.[25]

What about when your own children—who are supposed to be sleeping—start crying during the small group? Make sure you and your wife have a strategy for taking care of them. Which of you will leave in the middle of the small group lesson when one of them starts crying? Just make sure one of you is assigned to this task.

Think about IT!

Checklist to Avoid Distractions

- Is the ringer off on the Telephones?
- Is the temperature approximately 67 degrees?
- Are the seats arranged in a circle?
- Are there enough seats?
- Is sufficient light in the room?
- Are there enough song sheets? Bibles?

Time to Start

A common frustration among small group leaders is getting groups started on time. It's not unusual to wait five or ten minutes past the scheduled starting time while waiting for small group members to arrive.

The leader must decide. Will the group start on time or wait for the last few members to arrive? Two simple steps can help leaders conquer this age-old problem.[26]

Agree on expectations. Ask the group what they think about starting on time. This is the ideal time for the group to establish clear expectations concerning the starting time, and the importance (or unimportance) of group members arriving on time. Most likely, the group members will agree that arriving on time is important. The most important principle is agreement among group members. Remember also that you can continually review this commitment when new people are added.

Begin on time. Perhaps it seems obvious that the leader should start the group on time when battling chronic lateness. However, as mentioned earlier, many leaders don't start on time because they're waiting for all the participants to arrive. Delaying the beginning of group time sends several mixed signals to group members:

- "This meeting really doesn't start at 6:30; it starts at 6:45."
- "It's OK if I arrive late; they won't start without me anyway."
- "The first 15 minutes of our meeting isn't important."

If a small group leader begins on time regardless of latecomers, she's sending the signal that every part of the meeting is important. The leader is also making wise use of the limited time that's available for the meeting. Ultimately, if a small group leader is in the habit of starting on time, people will arrive on time. Conversely, if a leader does not start on time, the members will arrive later and later.

Try IT!

Read 1 Timothy 4:12

- What advice does Paul give Timothy in these verses?

____

____

____

____

- How can you apply "being an example" to starting the group on time?

____

____

____

____

Time to Close

I believe a small group meeting should not last longer than 1 ½ hours. I like to say to small group leaders: *If you don't strike oil in 1 ½ hours, stop boring.* David Cho, senior pastor of the Yoido Full Gospel Church, recommends that a small group meeting last no longer than one hour.

Small group members have a host of responsibilities, which include going to work, spending time with family, and completing numerous chores. A small group member might think twice about attending the next week if the meeting is too long.

Try IT!

- Formally End the Small group on Time
- Stand, hold hands in a circle and lead in a prayer of conclusion at the stated ending time—even if you're in the middle of something! Don't wear out your welcome, especially among those who have children and need the time to prepare for the next day. The weekly small group gathering is only one small part of small group life. The balance must be lived out in homes and relationships all week long!

God's Blessing on Your Home

With all these details, you might feel hesitant about hosting a small group. Before saying no, consider God's blessing upon your home.

When someone opens his home for a small group, the Spirit of God is invited to reign in that house. God will certainly honor your step of faith and abundantly bless your house and all that you have. Consider what he did for Obed-Edom.

In 2 Samuel 6:10-12, we read how God blessed the house of Obed-Edom because of the presence of the ark of the God:

> He [David] was not willing to take the ark of the LORD to be with him in the City of David. Instead, he took it aside to the house of Obed-Edom the Gittite. 11 The ark of the LORD remained in the house of Obed-Edom the Gittite for three months, and the LORD blessed him and his entire household. 12 Now King David was told, "The LORD has blessed the household of Obed-Edom and everything he has, because of the ark of God." So David went down and brought up the ark of God from the house of Obed-Edom to the City of David with rejoicing.

Opening your home for a small group doesn't require God to bless your home. He is, however, present as promised in Matthew 18:20 "For where two or three come together in my name, there am I". You will, through the group worship, prayers, and study of Scripture, be allowing the living God to bless you and your home.

Small group leaders with 20-20 vision see distractions before they become stumbling blocks to a successful meeting. While concentrating on the larger issues, successful leaders don't neglect the details.

Do IT!

Work out an agreement or covenant about when to start the group, refreshments to bring, and when to close the group.

Memorize IT!

"Just as the Son of Man did not come to be served, but to serve, and to give his life as a ransom for many" (Matthew 20:28).

Remember it!

1. What was the main truth you learned from this lesson?
2. Main points:
    - The home atmosphere plays an important role in attracting and maintaining small group members.
    - Prevent distractions by preparing for them.
    - Children are an essential part of the small group and must receive ministry.

Apply it!

1. Arrange the seating in a circle.
2. Provide song sheets for everyone in the group.
3. Make sure there's sufficient light in the room.
4. Start on time and close on time.

Chapter Notes

Chapter Notes

Endnotes

[1] As small group size increases there is a direct decrease of equally distributed participation. In other words, the difference in the percentage of remarks between the most active person and the least active person becomes greater and greater as the small group size increases [John K. Brilhart, *Effective Group Discussion* 4th ed. (Dubuque, Iowa: Wm. C. Brown Company Publishers, 1982), p. 59].

[2] Touch Publications sells a book dedicated entirely to icebreakers (call 1-800-735-5865 or go to www.touchusa.org) NavPress sells an excellent book called *101 Best Small Group Ideas* (Colorado Springs, CO: NavPress Publishing Group, 1996; http://www.navpress.com/. The Serendipity Bible is loaded with excellent icebreaker questions: http://www.serendipityhouse.com/pages/home.html

[3] The following points were taken from an article by Dan Smith and Steven Reames entitled, "Leading Worship in Small Groups," *Small Group Dynamics* (Small Group Network, September 1999).

[4] This small group took place in Liberia, West Africa during a short term mission trip in 1982.

[5] Admittedly, not all small groups focus on participation as I'm promoting in this book. Small group leaders at Yoido Full Gospel Church, the Elim Church, and the International Charismatic Mission teach the small group lesson. They do not see themselves as facilitators as much as preachers and teachers. I would not equate these small groups as "Bible studies" because these small groups focus on non-Christians just as much as believers. Small groups in other small group churches do promote participation. Ralph Neighbour, for example, has done more than anyone I know to promote group participation in small groups. The small groups at Faith Community Baptist Church in Singapore, the church that Ralph Neighbour helped establish, are 100% participatory. Even before I imbibed the cell church philosophy, I wholeheartedly promoted group participation and the small group leader as facilitator rather than Bible teacher.

[6] David Hocking, *The Seven Laws of Christian Leadership* (Ventura, CA: Regal Books, 1991), p. 63.

[7] Ralph Neighbour Jr., "Questions and Answers," *Cell Church magazine*, Vol 2., No. 4, 1993, p. 2.

[8] The Art of Mentoring: Lead, Follow, and Get Out of the Way (Houston, TX: Bullion Books, 1998), p. 46.

[9] Howard A.Snyder, *The Radical Wesley & Patterns for Church Renewal* (Downers Grove, IL: Inter-Varsity Press, 1980), p. 55.

[10] Judy Hamlin, *The Small Group Leader's Training Course* (Colorado Springs, CO: NavPress, 1990), pp. 54-57

[11] The 7 Habits of Highly Effective People, New York: Simon and Schuster, 1989, p. 239.

[12] Michael Mack, "Kinesics," *Small Group Dynamics* (Small Group Network. [n.d.]).

[13] Judy Hamlin, *The Small Group Leader's Training Course* (Colorado Springs, CO: NavPress, 1990), pp. 51-80.

[14] Ralph Neighbour, "Jesus is the Real Cell Leader," *Small Group Dynamics* (Small Group Network, January 2000).

[15] Roberta Hestenes, *Using the Bible in Groups* (Philadelphia: The Westminster Press, 1983), p. 29.

[16] Charles D. Meigs, "Lord, help me live from day to day" (Hymn, 1902).

[17] Henry, Matthew, *Matthew Henry's Commentary on the Bible* (Peabody, MA: Hendrickson Publishers) 1997.

[18] B.A. Fisher & J. Winke, "You Always Hurt the One You Love: Strategies and Tactics in Interpersonal Conflict," *Communication Quarterly*, 27, no.1. (Winter 1979): 3-11 as quoted in Julie A. Gorman *Community that is Christian: A Handbook on Small Groups* (Wheaton, ILL: Victor Books, 1993), p. 195.

[19] Barbara J. Fleischer, *Facilitating for Growth* (Collegeville, MN: The Liturgical Press, 1993), p. 84.

[20] *Cell Church Magazine*, Summer, 1996, p. 11.

[21] Michael Mack, "Top 10 Ways to Facilitate so Your Group Can Participate" *Cell Church Magazine* Vol. 8, no.2 (Spring 1999): 22-25. I'm grateful to Michael Mack's article for providing the ideas behind the sub-headings used in this chapter. I also included some of his material from that excellent article.

[22] I don't buy the argument that says you need to have an expensive home to open a small group. If you live in a lower-class area, most likely the majority of the home will be like yours. Neighbors will be glad to attend. Even with homogeneous groups, it's likely that you'll invite "your kind of people" (people of your social status, background, etc.). I don't buy the argument that says you need to have an expensive home to open a small group.

[23] Wayne Meeks, *The First Urban Christians: The Social World of the Apostle Paul* (New Haven, CT: Yale University Press, 1983), p. 29, as quoted in Hae Gyue Kim, *Biblical Foundations for the Cell-Based Churches Applied to the Urban Context of Seoul, Korea* (Pasadena, CA: Fuller Theological Seminary, 2003), p. 89.

[24] My book, *Children in Cell Ministry* (CCS Publishing, 2016) is available at www.joelcomiskeygroup.com or by calling 1-888-511-9995.

[25] One time I was consulting with a small group of Christian leaders. The wife kept on jumping up and answering the telephone.. I felt like my advice wasn't very important—like her next phone call was far more important. Small group leader; now project this to your members. They won't feel important if you're prioritizing the telephone, your computer, or your dog over them.

[26] The principles behind this list were taken from an article by Mark Whelchel entitled "Chronic Lateness," *Small Group Dynamics* (Small Group Network, June 1999).

RESOURCES
BY
JOEL COMISKEY

You can find all of Joel Comiskey's books at:
www.joelcomiskeygroup.com
Phone: 1-888-511-9995
email: joelcomiskeyinfo@gmail.com

Joel Comiskey's previous books cover the following topics

• Leading a cell group (*How to Lead a Great Cell Group Meeting*, 2001, 2009; *Children in Cell Ministry*, 2016; *Youth in Cell Ministry*, 2016).

• How to multiply the cell group (*Home Cell Group Explosion*, 1998).

• How to prepare spiritually for cell ministry (*An Appointment with the King*, 2002, 2011).

• How to practically organize your cell system (*Reap the Harvest*, 1999; *Cell Church Explosion*, 2004).

• How to train future cell leaders (*Leadership Explosion*, 2001; *Live*, 2007; *Encounter*, 2007; *Grow*, 2007; *Share*, 2007; *Lead*, 2007; *Coach*, 2008; *Discover*, 2008).

• How to coach/care for cell leaders (*How to be a Great Cell Group Coach*, 2003; *Groups of Twelve*, 2000; *From Twelve to Three*, 2002).

• How the gifts of the Spirit work within the cell group (*The Spirit-filled Small Group*, 2005, 2009; *Discover*, 2008).

• How to fine tune your cell system (*Making Cell Groups Work Navigation Guide*, 2003).

• Principles from the second largest church in the world (*Passion and Persistence*, 2004).

• How cell church works in North America (*The Church that Multiplies*, 2007, 2009).

• How to plant a church (*Planting Churches that Reproduce*, 2009)

• How to be a relational disciple (*Relational Disciple*, 2010).

• How to distinguish truth from myths (*Myths and Truths of the Cell Church*, 2011).

• What the Biblical foundations for cell church are (*Biblical Foundations for the Cell-Based Church*, 2012, *Making Disciples in the Cell-Based Church*, 2013, *2000 Years of Small Groups*, 2015).

All of the books listed are available from Joel Comiskey Group

www.joelcomiskeygroup.com

How To Lead A Great Cell Group Meeting:

So People Want to Come Back

Do people expectantly return to your group meetings every week? Do you have fun and experience joy during your meetings? Is everyone participating in discussion and ministry? You can lead a great cell group meeting, one that is life changing and dynamic. Most people don't realize that they can create a God-filled atmosphere because they don't know how. Now the secret is out. This guide will show you how to:

- Prepare yourself spiritually to hear God during the meeting
- Structure the meeting so it flows
- Spur people in the group to participate and share their lives openly
- Share your life with others in the group
- Create stimulating questions
- Listen effectively to discover what is transpiring in others' lives
- Encourage and edify group members
- Open the group to non-Christians
- See the details that create a warm atmosphere

By implementing these time-tested ideas, your group meetings will become the hot-item of your members' week. They will go home wanting more and return each week bringing new people with them. 140 pgs.

Home Cell Group Explosion:
How Your Small Group Can Grow and Multiply

The book crystallizes the author's findings in some eighteen areas of research, based on a meticulous questionnaire that he submitted to cell church leaders in eight countries around the world, locations that he also visited personally for his research. The detailed notes in the back of the book offer the student of cell church growth a rich mine for further reading. The beauty of Comiskey's book is that he not only summarizes his survey results in a thoroughly convincing way but goes on to analyze in practical ways many of his survey results in separate chapters. The happy result is that any cell church leader, intern or member completing this quick read will have his priorities/values clearly aligned and ready to be followed-up. If you are a pastor or small group leader, you should devour this book! It will encourage you and give you simple, practical steps for dynamic small group life and growth. 175 pgs.

An Appointment with the King:
Ideas for Jump-Starting Your Devotional Life

With full calendars and long lists of things to do, people often put on hold life's most important goal: building an intimate relationship with God. Often, believers wish to pursue the goal but are not sure how to do it. They feel frustrated or guilty when their attempts at personal devotions seem empty and unfruitful. With warm, encouraging writing, Joel Comiskey guides readers on how to set a daily appointment with the King and make it an exciting time they will look forward to. This book first answers the question "Where do I start?" with step-by-step instructions on how to spend time with God and practical ideas for experiencing him more fully. Second, it highlights the benefits of spending time with God, including joy, victory over sin, and spiritual guidance. The book will help Christians tap into God's resources on a daily basis, so that even in the midst of busyness they can walk with him in intimacy and abundance. 175 pgs.

Reap the Harvest:
How a Small Group System Can Grow System Can Grow Your Church

Have you tried small groups and hit a brick wall? Have you wondered why your groups are not producing the fruit that was promised? Are you looking to make your small groups more effective? Cell-church specialist and pastor Dr. Joel Comiskey studied the world's most successful cell churches to determine why they grow. The key: They have embraced specific principles. Conversely, churches that do not embrace these same principles have problems with their groups and therefore do not grow. Cell churches are successful not because they have small groups but because they can support the groups. In this book, you will discover how these systems work. 236 pgs.

La Explosión de la Iglesia Celular:
Cómo Estructurar la Iglesia en Células Eficaces (Editorial Clie, 2004)

This book is available only in Spanish and contains Joel Comiskey's research of eight of the world's largest cell churches, five of which reside in Latin America. It details how to make the transition from a traditional church to the cell church structure and many other valuable insights, including: the history of the cell church, how to organize your church to become a praying church, the most important principles of the cell church, and how to raise up an army of cell leaders. 236 pgs.

Leadership Explosion:
Multiplying Cell Group Leaders to Reap the Harvest

Some have said that cell groups are leader breeders. Yet even the best cell groups often have a leadership shortage. This shortage impedes growth and much of the harvest goes untouched. Joel Comiskey has discovered why some churches are better at raising up new cell leaders than others. These churches do more than pray and hope for new leaders. They have an intentional strategy, a plan that will quickly equip as many new leaders as possible. In this book, you will discover the training models these churches use to multiply leaders. You will discover the underlying principles of these models so that you can apply them. 202 pgs.

FIVE-BOOK EQUIPPING SERIES

#1: Live **#2: Encounter** **#3: Grow** **#4: Share** **#5: Lead**

The five book equipping series is designed to train a new believer all the way to leading his or her own cell group. Each of the five books contains eight lessons. Each lesson has interactive activities that helps the trainee reflect on the lesson in a personal, practical way.

Live starts the training by covering key Christian doctrines, including baptism and the Lord's supper. 85 pgs.

Encounter guides the believer to receive freedom from sinful bondages. The Encounter book can be used one-on-one or in a group. 91 pgs.

Grow gives step-by-step instruction for having a daily quiet time, so that the believer will be able to feed him or herself through spending daily time with God. 87 pgs.

Share instructs the believer how to communicate the gospel message in a winsome, personal way. This book also has two chapters on small group evangelism. 91 pgs.

Lead prepares the Christian on how to facilitate an effective cell group. This book would be great for those who form part of a small group team. 91 pgs.

TWO-BOOK ADVANCED TRAINING SERIES

Coach and **Discover** make-up the Advanced Training, prepared specifically to take a believer to the next level of maturity in Christ.

Coach prepares a believer to coach another cell leader. Those experienced in cell ministry often lack understanding on how to coach someone else. This book provides step-by-step instruction on how to coach a new cell leader from the first meeting all the way to giving birth to a new group. The book is divided into eight lessons, which are interactive and help the potential coach deal with real-life, practical coaching issues. 85 pgs.

Discover clarifies the twenty gifts of the Spirit mentioned in the New Testament. The second part shows the believer how to find and use his or her particular gift. This book is excellent to equip cell leaders to discover the giftedness of each member in the group. 91 pgs.

How to be a Great Cell Group Coach:
Practical insight for Supporting and Mentoring Cell Group Leaders

Research has proven that the greatest contributor to cell group success is the quality of coaching provided for cell group leaders. Many are serving in the position of a coach, but they don't fully understand what they are supposed to do in this position. Joel Comiskey has identified seven habits of great cell group coaches. These include: Receiving from God, Listening to the needs of the cell group leader, Encouraging the cell group leader, Caring for the multiple aspects of a leader's life, Developing the cell leader in various aspects of leadership, Strategizing with the cell leader to create a plan, Challenging the cell leader to grow.

Practical insights on how to develop these seven habits are outlined in section one. Section two addresses how to polish your skills as a coach with instructions on diagnosing problems in a cell group, how to lead coaching meetings, and what to do when visiting a cell group meeting. This book will prepare you to be a great cell group coach, one who mentors, supports, and guides cell group leaders into great ministry. 139 pgs.

Groups of Twelve:
A New Way to Mobilize Leaders and Multiply Groups in Your Church

This book clears the confusion about the Groups of 12 model. Joel dug deeply into the International Charismatic Mission in Bogota, Colombia and other G12 churches to learn the simple principles that

G12 has to offer your church. This book also contrasts the G12 model with the classic 5x5 and shows you what to do with this new model of ministry. Through onsite research, international case studies, and practical experience, Joel Comiskey outlines the G12 principles that your church can use today.

Billy Hornsby, director of the Association of Related Churches, says, "Joel Comiskey shares insights as a leader who has himself raised up numerous leaders. From how to recognize potential leaders to cell leader training to time-tested principles of leadership—this book has it all. The accurate comparisons of various training models make it a great resource for those who desire more leaders. Great book!" 182 pgs.

From Twelve To Three:

How to Apply G12 Principles in Your Church

The concept of the Groups of 12 began in Bogota, Colombia, but now it is sweeping the globe. Joel Comiskey has spent years researching the G12 structure and the principles behind it.

From his experience as a pastor, trainer, and consultant, he has discovered that there are two ways to embrace the G12 concept: adopting the entire model or applying the principles that support the model.

This book focuses on the application of principles rather than adoption of the entire model. It outlines the principles and provides a modified application which Joel calls the G12.3. This approach presents a pattern that is adaptable to many different church contexts.

The concluding section illustrates how to implement the G12.3 in various kinds of churches, including church plants, small churches, large churches, and churches that already have cells. 178 pgs.

The Spirit-filled Small Group:

Leading Your Group to Experience the Spiritual Gifts.

The focus in many of today's small groups has shifted from Spirit-led transformation to just another teacher-student Bible study. But exercising every member's spiritual gifts is vital to the effectiveness of the group. With insight born of experience in more than twenty years of small group ministry, Joel Comiskey explains how leaders and participants alike can be supernaturally equipped to deal with real-life issues. Put these principles into practice and your small group will never be the same!

This book works well with Comiskey's training book, Discover. It fleshes out many of the principles in Comiskey's training book. Chuck Crismier, radio host, Viewpoint, writes, "Joel Comiskey has again provided the Body of Christ with an important tool to see God's Kingdom revealed in and through small groups." 191 pgs.

Making Cell Groups Work Navigation Guide:

A Toolbox of Ideas and Strategies for Transforming Your Church.

For the first time, experts in cell group ministry have come together to provide you with a page reference tool like no other. When Ralph Neighbour, Bill Beckham, Joel Comiskey and Randall Neighbour compiled new articles and information under careful orchestration and in-depth understanding that Scott Boren brings to the table, it's as powerful as private consulting! Joel Comiskey has an entire book within this mammoth page work. There are also four additional authors.

Passion and Persistence:

How the Elim Church's Cell Groups Penetrated an Entire City for Jesus

This book describes how the Elim Church in San Salvador grew from a small group to 116,000 people in 10,000 cell groups. Comiskey takes the principles from Elim and applies them to churches in North America and all over the world.

Ralph Neighbour says: "I believe this book will be remember as one of the most important ever written about a cell church movement! I experienced the passion when visiting Elim many years ago. Comiskey's report about Elim is not a pattern to be slavishly copied. It is a journey into grasping the true theology and methodology of the New Testament church. You'll discover how the Elim Church fans into flame their passion for Jesus and His Word, how they organize their cells to penetrate a city and world for Jesus, and how they persist until God brings the fruit." 158 pgs.

The Church that Multiplies:

Growing a Healthy Cell Church in North America

Does the cell church strategy work in North America? We hear about exciting cell churches in Colombia and Korea, but where are the dynamic North American cell churches? This book not only declares that the cell church concept does work in North America but dedicates an entire chapter to examining North American churches that are successfully using the cell strategy to grow in quality and quantity. This book provides the latest statistical research about the North American church and explains why the cell church approach restores health and growth to the church today. More than anything else, this book will provide practical solutions for pastors and lay leaders to use in implementing cell-based ministry. 181 pgs.

Planting Churches that Reproduce:
Planting a Network of Simple Churches

What is the best way to plant churches in the 21st century? Comiskey believes that simple, reproducible church planting is most effective. The key is to plant churches that are simple enough to grow into a movement of churches. Comiskey has been gathering material for this book for the past fifteen Years. He has also planted three churches in a wide variety of settings.

Planting Churches that Reproduce is the fruit of his research and personal experience. Comiskey uses the latest North American church planting statistics, but extends the illustrations to include worldwide church planting. More than anything else, this book will provide practical solutions for those planting churches today. Comiskey's book is a must-read book for all those interested in establishing Christ-honoring, multiplying churches. 176 pgs.

The Relational Disciple:
How God Uses Community to Shape Followers of Jesus

Jesus lived with His disciples for three years and taught them life lessons as a group. After three years, he commanded them to "go and do likewise" (Matthew 28:18-20). Jesus discipled His followers through relationships—and He wants us to do the same. Scripture is full of exhortations to love and serve one another. This book will show you how. The isolation present in the western world is creating a hunger for community and the world is longing to see relational disciples in action. This book will encourage Christ-followers to allow God to use the natural relationships in life—family, friends, work relationships, cells, church, and missions to mold them into relational disciples.

You Can Coach:
How to Help Leaders Build Healthy Churches through Coaching

We've entitled this book "You Can Coach" because we believe that coaching is more about passing on what you've lived and holding thers accountable in the process. Coaching doesn't require a higher degree, special talent, unique personality, or a particular spiritual gift. We believe, in fact, that God wants coaching to become a movement. We long to see the day in which every pastor has a coach and in turn is coaching someone else. In this book, you'll hear three coaches who have successfully coached pastors for many years. They will share their history, dreams, principles, and what God is doing through coaching. Our hope is that you'll be both inspired and resourced to continue your own coaching ministry in the years to come.

Myths & Truths of the Cell Church:
Key Principles that Make or Break Cell Ministry

Most of the modern day cell church movement is dynamic, positive, and applicable. As is true in most endeavors, errors and false assumptions have also cropped up to destroy an otherwise healthy movement. Sometimes these false concepts caused the church to go astray completely. At other times, they led the pastor and church down a dead-end road of fruitless ministry. Regardless of how the myths were generated, they had a chilling effect on the church's ministry. In this book, Joel Comiskey tackles these errors and false assumptions, helping pastors and leaders to untangle the webs of legalism that has crept into the cell church movement. Joel then guides the readers to apply biblical, time-tested principles that will guide them into fruitful cell ministry. Each chapter begins with a unique twist. Well-known worldwide cell church leaders open each chapter by answering questions to the chapter's topic in the form of an email dialogue. Whether you're starting out for the first time in cell ministry or a seasoned veteran, this book will give you the tools to help your ministry stay fresh and fruitful.

Biblical Foundations for the Cell-Based Church

Why cell church? Is it because David Cho's church is a cell church and happens to be the largest church in the history of Christianity? Is it because cell church is the strategy that many "great" churches are using?

Ralph Neighbour repeatedly says, "Theology must breed methodology." Joel Comiskey has arrived at the same conclusion. Biblical truth is the only firm foundation for anything we do. Without a biblical base, we don't have a strong under-pinning upon which we can hang our ministry and philosophy. We can plod through most anything when we know that God is stirring us to behave biblically.

Making Disciples in the Cell-Based Church

The primary goal of the church is to make disciples who make disciples. But how is the church supposed to do that? This book answers that question. Dr. Comiskey explains how both cell and celebration (larger gathering) work together in the process of making disciples. In the cell, a potential disciple is transformed through community, priesthood of all believers, group evangelism, and team multiplication. The cell system ensures each leader has a coach and that training happens. Then the cells gather together to worship and grow through the teaching of God's Word. This book will help you understand why and how to become a church that prioritizes discipleship.

What others are saying: I've read all of Joel Comiskey's books, but this one is his best work yet. I'm looking forward to having all of our pastors, coaches, cell leaders and members read this book in the near future. *Dr. Dennis Watson, Lead Pastor, Celebration Church of New Orleans*

I am so excited about Joel Comiskey's new book, Making Disciples in the Twenty-First Century Church. Joel has unpacked discipleship, not just as an endeavor for individuals, but as the critical element for creating a church community and culture that reproduces the Kingdom of God all over the earth. *Jimmy Seibert, Senior Pastor, Antioch Community Church* Like Joel's other books, this one is solidly biblical, highly practical, wonderfully accessible and is grounded in Joel's vast research and experience. *Dr. Dave Earley, Lead Pastor, Grace City Church of Las Vegas, Nevada*

2000 Years of Small Groups: *A History of Cell Ministry in the Church*

This book explores how God has used small groups throughout church history, specifically focusing on the early church to the present time. God not only established the early church as a house to house movement, but he also has used small groups throughout church history. This book chronicles the small group or cell movement from Jesus all the way to the modern day cell explosion. Themes include:Small Groups In Biblical History, Small Groups In Early Christian History, Small Groups and Monasticism, Small Groups During the Pre-Reformation Period, Luther and Small Groups, Martin Bucer and Small Groups, The Anabaptist Movement, Puritan Conventicles, Pietism, The Moravians, The Methodists, Modern House Churches, Small Groups in North America, and The Modern Day Cell Church. This book will both critique the strengths and weaknesses of these historical movements and apply principles to today's church.

Children in Cell Ministry: *Discipling the Future Generation Now*

Joel Comiskey challenges pastors and leaders to move from simply educating children to forming them into disciples who make disciples. Comiskey lays out the Biblical base for children's ministry and then encourages pastors and leaders to formulate their own vision and philosophy for ministry to children based on the Biblical text. Comiskey highlights how to disciple children in both the large group and the small group. He quickly moves into practical examples of intergenerational cell groups and how effective cell churches have implemented this type of group. He then writes about children only cell groups, citing many practical examples from some of the most effective cell churches in the world. Comiskey covers equipping for children, how to equip the parents, and mistakes in working with children in the cell church. This book will help those wanting to minister to children both in large and small groups.

Youth in Cell Ministry: *Discipling the Future Generation*

If we are going to have a victorious church tomorrow, we must focus on the youth today. In this book, Comiskey lays out the biblical base for youth ministry, highlights the felt needs of today's youth, and then shows why small groups are the most effective way to make youth disciples today. Comiskey explains the difference between inter-generational cells and student-led groups, the equipping process for youth leaders, how to coach leaders, and how to get started in youth cell ministry. Comiskey also describes common errors in youth ministry and how to avoid them. This book is a must-read for all those wanting to make youth disciples through cell ministry.

Groups that Thrive

Why are some small groups dynamic, attractive, and breathe the life of Christ? Why do other groups stagnate and close? In this ground-breaking book, Joel Comiskey and Jim Egli describe eight surprises about thriving small groups from their research of 4800 small group participants on four continents.

The authors expose common small group assumptions and offer practical advice to group members and leaders to help their groups thrive. The book covers topics such as small group participation, the influence of food, worship, and how thriving small groups effectively reach others for Jesus Christ. Read this book if you want your group to grow healthier and thrive with new life.

www.ingramcontent.com/pod-product-compliance
Lightning Source LLC
Chambersburg PA
CBHW070804050426
42452CB00012B/2490

* 9 7 8 1 9 3 5 7 8 9 9 5 6 *